Don Aslett answers . . .

HOW DO I CLEAN THE MOOSEHEAD?

and 99 More Tough Questions About Housecleaning

DON ASLETT

Illustrated by Robert L. Betty

A PLUME BOOK

NEW AMERICAN LIBRARY

NEW YORK
PUBLISHED IN CANADA BY
PENGUIN BOOKS CANADA LIMITED, MARKHAM, ONTARIO

Acknowledgments

Bagging a moose isn't easy alone and writing a book only less so. Even with my thirty-two years of intense cleaning experience it took a good seasoned crew to do it. The champion moose caller and guide on the hunt to help me bag more of America's dirt was Gary Luke, executive editor at New American Library; the tanning and curing of the hide was done by my longtime editor and new agent Carol Cartaino; Mark Browning, professional cleaning consultant, mapped the way and kept us on target; Tobi Haynes, my production manager, brought it all together and mounted it perfectly; and our two alert scouts, Della Gibbs and Linda Hegg, tracked down those elusive missing bits of information. And we couldn't forget the man who added the all-important visual dimension, artist "Bert" Betty.

NAL BOOKS ARE AVAILABLE AT QUANTITY DISCOUNTS
WHEN USED TO PROMOTE PRODUCTS OR SERVICES.
FOR INFORMATION PLEASE WRITE TO PREMIUM MARKETING
DIVISION, NEW AMERICAN LIBRARY, 1633 BROADWAY,
NEW YORK, NEW YORK 10019.

Published simultaneously in Canada by Penguin Books Canada Limited.

PLUME TRADEMARK REG. U.S. PAT. OFF. AND FOREIGN COUNTRIES
REGISTERED TRADEMARK—MARCA REGISTRADA
HECHO EN DRESDEN, TN, U.S.A.

SIGNET, SIGNET CLASSIC, MENTOR, ONYX, PLUME, MERIDIAN and NAL BOOKS
are published in the United States by New American Library,
a division of Penguin Books USA Inc., 1633 Broadway, New York, New York 10019,
in Canada by Penguin Books Canada Limited, 2801 John Street,
Markham, Ontario L3R 1B4

Designed by Barbara Huntley

First Printing, September, 1989

1 2 3 4 5 6 7 8 9

PRINTED IN THE UNITED STATES OF AMERICA

Contents

Introduction

When it comes to cleaning, everyone has a question. Whether we're a fussy housekeeper or a "lick and promise" cleaner, there are always those large and small cleaning projects that frustrate, puzzle, elude, baffle, worry, annoy, discourage, and mystify us. Plus the ones where we just don't know where to start.

People ask more questions about cleaning than about the weather, politics, the basketball averages, and the latest celebrity combined. The reason is simple: We all have to clean, and there aren't a lot of experts on the subject around, so few of the whats, whens, whys, and hows of cleaning have really been answered so far.

When I wrote *Is There Life After Housework?* I figured I'd answered everyone's questions about cleaning. That book of answers sold more than one-half million copies in six other questioning continents, as well as the U.S. When it became clear that *Life After Housework* didn't get all the wondering out of cleaning, I collected the continuing inquiries and answered one hundred of them in a book called *Do I Dust or Vacuum First?* It too became a favorite among homemakers, reviewers, and media interviewers everywhere. Could there be any more questions? Could there? Are you kidding?

Not only more, but tougher and better questions have flowed in since 1982, when *Do I Dust or Vacuum First?* made its debut. People have kept on sending, calling, and bringing them in. More questions and better questions could only mean one thing—another and a better book of answers. (This time I'll even answer the rest of the questions my editor wanted me to answer in the *last* book!)

So here with even more professional cleaners' secrets and shortcuts for the homemaker are the next one hundred most-asked questions. Questions always make life interesting, and I hope these particular answers also make life around home a little easier.

How can I get started cleaning? #1

You're not going to the dentist, just doing a little cleaning. You can listen to some country and western or classical music while you're doing it or solve the problems of the universe in your mind as you go. The more practice you get cleaning, the easier it becomes.

Somehow I don't think I've convinced you yet to start cleaning, so let me share some startup strategies from people who can't wait to start any project—even cleaning.

Don't try to do it all at once. The first truth of housework is that it's repetitious. So break up the cleaning up—instead of a big, long marathon every Saturday, which you dread all week and feel sorry for yourself all during, do a half hour or an hour a day; it'll go twice as fast, and you'll enjoy it more.

Don't let yourself be put on the defensive! We let a lot of housework get to the crisis point before we decide to handle it. Who could like it or want to do it then? We let a little bit of cleaning go until the mess multiplies and demoralizes us. A dish or two is almost pleasant to do until it becomes a whole double sink and counter and tabletop and oven full of clotted cereal bowls and greasy broiler pans and hardened chili plates. Then it's a crisis and we don't want to have to deal with it. Don't wait . . . the mess won't dematerialize!

Concentrate on the end result. The promise of success and reward is the big secret of "getting around to it" in anything. All we need is confidence in the outcome. Cleaning is just a preliminary to enjoying order and organization. Being able to sit in the midst of a clean, attractive environment you've created is a great thrill.

Here are some more "getting-started" ideas:

• Have a good, efficient set of cleaning tools and keep them sharp and handy. You won't risk losing your ambition before you find the bowl brush, and second-rate stuff makes us feel a little discouraged and second-rate.

• Change into your "cleaning uniform." Clothes help create the mood for many an undertaking, and cleaning is no exception. When we get our sweats or our serious cleaning clothes on, we know it's time to roll up our sleeves and roll.

• Do your get-set ritual, whatever it may be, from washing your face to remaking your list, moving the furniture out of the way, or pouring a hot cup of whatever.

• Start early—no later than 9:00 in the **morning** is best, but even early in the evening, if that's when it has to be, will help. Don't give your will a chance to wind down.

• Get a couple of machines going—the dishwasher, the vacuum, the clothes washer, even the fan in the bathroom. It'll create a momentum.

• Bribe yourself, shame yourself, prod yourself, trick yourself—do **anything** you have to do to just get launched into the actual doing. (It's all downhill from there, as we know.)

• Decide what you're going to do the night/day/week before. Then you can just jump in and start doing it, rather than be bogged down in agonizing and debating over what and when.

• Promise yourself and **keep** the promise that quitting time is____. We don't mind enlisting so much if we know for sure when we'll get out.

2

• Start with something you like . . . the thing you actually **do** enjoy cleaning . . . especially if it cleans up fast or shines afterward.

• Combine a cleaning chore with something you like, like talking on the phone. Say to yourself, "I'll call Carol and talk until the counters are cleared and cleaned." This'll work even better if you have a phone in every room.

• Start with something that's highly visible, that everyone will notice immediately.

• Give yourself an audience. Start with something that has to be done outside, or find a friend who's at least willing to trail you around and talk.

• If it's a big job, break it down into pieces and focus cheerfully on the fact that you only have to do stage ____ today.

• Get mad: If you need a little help with this, stand on the scales, balance the checkbook, or look in the kids' room or your husband's closet. Adrenaline will pour in to the aid of the cleaning impulse!

• If all else fails, invite company for sometime soon.

All I ever seem to have is bits and snatches of time. How can I get any housework done that way ? #2

Half of the people who look at this see an upright vacuum; the other half see two people talking it out. Likewise, some people fit life in around housework; others, like me for example, fit all housework around life. I never use prime time to clean and maintain. I do it all in bits and snatches—one-, two-, and ten-minute time segments that might otherwise be wasted. I always pick up and neaten up while I'm walking through or on my way somewhere. I always clean the area around the phone while I'm talking on it, always clean the car while the gas is pumping in, always clean the kitchen while things are cooking, always clean my pockets waiting in airports—you do lots of this, too, I know—so just do a little more of it. My cleaning crews beat competitors because we never wait for wax to dry, latecomers to show, etc. We have a list of

4

what needs to be done and we always keep moving because in the course of a day ten five- or six-minute "lulls" or twenty three-minute "waits" add up to one hour and that can account for a lot of cleaning.

If you use quick professional methods you can clean two bathrooms while you're waiting for a tub to fill. And cleaning the light fixture when you have to get up there and change a bulb anyway eliminates a nuisance job later. All straightening up, all trash disposal, all dusting, all spot cleaning, and a lot of dejunking, can be done while on the way or while doing something else.

If they just cleaned during commercials the average TV watcher would have forty-eight minutes of extra time a day. Jumping up and down ninety-six times would eliminate the need for exercise class, too, so there's another hour saved. You could clean your two nearest neighbors' houses just for good measure—all in extra, unused, nonproductive time.

Don't forget that all windows, all floors, all walls—or for that matter all sides or parts of something—don't get dirty at the same time. Things actually get dirty in bits and snatches, so what could be a more logical way to clean them? Lots of things get dirtied in spare time, so it's only fair to use spare moments to restore them.

Play the bits game. Try it for at least a week and see what happens. Don't schedule or plan any cleaning—just slip it in whenever you see the chance. You'll never be the same, nor will your cleaning schedule. Focus on fun and living and do the cleaning on your way or in between—I guarantee you'll run out of housework before you run out of bits and snatches of time!

Here's a few fit-it-in favorites to get you started or to add to your odd-moments repertoire—in fact, each one of these tasks can be completed in the time span of a TV commercial break!

- Load or unload the dishwasher
- Hand-wash a sink full of dishes
- Clean out one drawer
- Wipe out the microwave
- Pretty up one appliance front
- Decrumb, despatter, and polish one small appliance
- Desmudge the kitchen cupboards
- Quick-clean the inside of the refrigerator
- Sponge down the high chair
- Declutter the entryway or the stairs
- Make a bed
- Shine one window or mirror or sliding glass door

5

- Polish one piece of furniture
- Dust or spray-clean the wall hangings
- Dust or clean the legs or bottom of something
- Pair some socks
- Dust mop or sweep a floor
- Dejunk the window sill or dressertop
- Clean off the top and sides of something
- Dust off the TV or stereo
- Put the scattered tapes, records, magazines, or newspapers away
- Hang up some flung clothes
- Wipe down some switchplates or door frames or one door
- Clean out the cat box
- Sort the mail
- Shake out one rug
- Wipe down or declutter one or two shelves
- Take out the trash

How often do I need to strip the floor 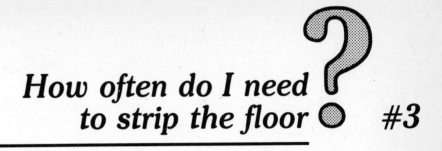 *#3*

Once is more than enough for most of us! This is a hard, sloppy job, so the longer we can legitimately put it off, the happier we'll be. The amount of use and abuse a vinyl or linoleum floor gets, more than time, determines stripping frequency. In general, you can tell more about when to strip by looking at the floor than at the calendar. I've seen floors go five years without stripping, while some need it every five months.

Stripping, which is removing all the old wax and dirt down to the bare floor, is necessary when:

• You've been wondering what happened to the pattern for a while now.

• The wax, especially around the edges of the floor, gets built up and unsightly.

• The wax is cloudy and dirty-looking from dirt embedded in it.

• The floor seems dull and discolored, even after you wash and rewax it.

• You've rewaxed at least eight times that you can remember.

The following are the best ways to **prevent** having to ever strip a floor too soon:

• Be sure to use a floor polish that says "nonyellowing" on the label.

• Don't use strong cleaners like Top Job or Mr. Clean on waxed surfaces. They dull the finish and even remove the wax—unevenly, unfortunately!

• If you limit your wax or floor finish applications, when you "rewax," to the traffic areas where it wears off and actually needs to be replaced, you'll strip a lot less often than your neighbor who waxes the corners, edges, and under things every time he takes the wax applicator out.

• Keep the floor swept and mopped, so dirt doesn't grind into the finish.

• Use good professional-quality doormats both inside and outside every doorway. (See p. 18)

• Be sure the floor is good and clean before you apply that initial—or a later—coat of wax. Waxing over dirt is the biggest single cause of premature stripping. It's usually better to grit your teeth and give the floor a thorough cleaning and then apply a professional-quality floor finish than to use a "clean and polish at the same time" product. That dirt has to go somewhere, and where could it be but into the wax?

• Don't apply wax too heavily when you do, or the excess will collect in all the low areas on the floor and begin to look awful in a hurry. If it runs and puddles when you're putting it on, it's too thick!

• If you like to apply a second coat when you wax, make sure the first coat is dry before you do. Wax dries from the top down, and it may seem dry to the touch but be soft underneath. A too-soon-applied second coat will dissolve that thin surface skin and pull the first coat partly loose as it gloms together with it. The result will be a ropy, seamy, ugly mess.

How can I make my marked up and scuffed up baseboards look better ? #4

For years now I've issued a challenge to home and commercial cleaners alike: find or invent a new baseboard that looks better and is easy to clean—and you'll be a millionaire!

Baseboards are the battering point of every home and business building—they're in a prime location for punishment, and they always look awful, especially the rubber or vinyl ones. They look good for about the first two hours after installation, and then they start collecting dust, hair, and dead flies. And our toes, heels, brooms, and vacuums scuff and mark them. Their appearance really undoes an otherwise shipshape room. Ditto for painted wood baseboards—as those black marks, nicks, and scratches mount up they really start to look tacky.

With every passing year I like "coved" carpeting (see illustration) and earth tile baseboards better than the vinyls, woods, and other delicate trim.

9

My first advice for dealing with old-style baseboards is to make sure the rubber guard or bumper on your cleaning machine (vacuum, buffer, etc.) is in place and functional. And make sure your other cleaning tools aren't the kind that will mark, cut, or stub the baseboard while you're cleaning the floor. And take it easy when you're using strong cleaning solutions and floor strippers—if you splash these chemicals around they'll splotch, yellow, or discolor the baseboards. Remember, too, that baseboard materials are soft; even most wooden ones are made of soft wood, which dents easily, so you have to tell Junior not to run his toy trucks into them at top speed. And yes, those black marks are tough to remove, but don't use steel wool or powdered cleanser on them or you'll dull and damage the finish and make it much harder to clean in the future. Use a little all-purpose cleaner in a spray bottle instead and a white nylon backed sponge. Keep the surface wet and rub firmly, and any residue should slide right off.

To restore tired-looking rubber or vinyl baseboards:

1. Clean them—first spray a good solution of wax stripper on and let it sit a couple of minutes to dissolve and loosen old wax and built-up soil and grime.

2. Scrub with a long-handled floor scrubber such as a Doodle Bug so you don't have to bend over. A nylon pad like this beats a scrub brush or steel wool ten to one. Then rinse those baseboards off. Older ones especially are likely to look dull and dried out, and some marks will still show a little.

3. Apply a light coat of floor finish to ease baseboard cleaning hereafter. It'll do a lot to hide the scrapes, renew the color, and bring some brilliance up—a little matter of light reflection. A waxed surface also helps repel debris and makes getting the black marks, the mop marks, the splattered catsup, and other sticky stuff off easier. It'll also blend or cover bleached out areas and offer a measure of protection to the surface itself. Just don't overdo your baseboard waxing to the point that you get a yellowed wax buildup on there. Remember, we never walk on a baseboard, so you don't need to wax it every time you wax the floor. And don't be indecisive about it—half waxing it and half not—or you'll end up with an ugly, uneven line that only adds to your baseboard blues.

Nicks and scratches on painted base can be filled with spackle or wood filler as necessary and touched up with a bit of matching paint. Schedule an overall painting every other year or so. Wiping your baseboards with a damp mop or cloth after that will be the best thing you can do to maintain them. Every time you do this you can work on your brilliant new baseboard design. I'll be the first buyer—at least 292 miles' worth!

Can I ruin things cleaning 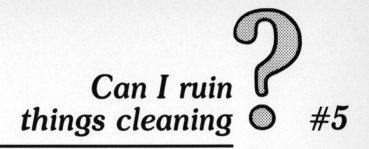 #5

You sure can—in fact, you could often call cleaning a form of vandalism. All of the scouring and chipping away at things we do in the course of our bathroom brightening, for example, does more to ruin a restroom than all of the toilet flushers and hand washers who use it. How can the users wear out a bathroom? They can't! It's we cleaners who pack the whittling-down-to-nothing wallop. How we clean and what we use to clean with has the biggest single impact on the life expectancy of our fixtures and furnishings. We slowly and sometimes not so slowly destroy the very things we're trying to preserve with:

Casually chosen chemicals. Our greatest allies in cleaning are chemicals, and they can work wonders, provided they're used on the right surface in the right concentration.

Acid bowl cleaners, for example, should never be used outside the toilet bowl, as they'll damage most metals and plastics. In fact, just setting the dripping bottle on your counter can leave a permanent ring. Chlorine bleach, used by many for general cleaning, is hazardous to the health of many household surfaces. It's a potent oxidizer that will even-

11

tually pit and discolor even the best chrome plating. Ammonia is a harsh alkaline cleaner that can alter dyes, dissolve varnish, and darken metal.

Overkill. Even mild chemicals and cleaning solutions used to excess can disintegrate, corrode, discolor, loosen glue and backing, split seams, and soften paint. Too much of anything is usually damaging as well as ineffective. It's always the gush of "extra" we put on that runs under the fridge or down into the cracks or the innards to rot, rust, stain, streak, shrink, mildew, and warp things. Double doses mean double trouble!

You even have to be careful with plain old water. There's no need to baptize the item you're cleaning—use a sane amount of solution to just slightly wet the surface. A discreet dampening cleans most things just as well as a flood job and leaves you with less swabbing up afterward.

Abrasive tools and cleaners. True, they do get the dirt off fast, but in the process they often take off or damage the finish of whatever we're cleaning. Steel wool or colored scrub pads or wire brushes will usually "get the job done," but leave you with a marred surface. Powdered cleansers will eventually scratch and dull most fixtures—even porcelain. Many a tub and sink has a porous, pitted surface that stains easily and is hard to clean because abrasive cleansers have worn away the slick protective finish. Even today's soft cleansers are nothing but a milder grade of abrasive—and must also be used with caution. And even the gentlest abrasives of all are fatal to very soft or shiny finishes such as clear plastic or stainless steel or mirror-finish aluminum.

Reckless wiping and scraping. A dry cloth or paper towel on a dry but still dirty surface will drag grit from one end of your fine finish to the other. And carelessly wielded putty knives and razor blades have marred more windows than they've ever removed cement drops, labels, or paint specks from. (Always wetting the surface first before you scrape will go a long way toward preventing scratches.)

Faulty equipment. A plain old vacuum with the bumper guard missing is more lethal to furniture legs and doors and the bottoms of cabinets than a convoy of kids with Tonka trucks. Mops, brooms, or squeegees with sharp points or protruding edges will scratch and snag and graze. A leaky bucket can ruin the finish on a nice wood floor, and ladders with the protective toeplates missing can easily gouge a hole in vinyl flooring.

So do a quick check of your cleaning chemicals and equipment and add a little caution to your cleaning routine. Reach for the gentlest cleaner first, instead of the strongest. And when in doubt, read the label. It'll add years to the life of your fixtures and furnishings.

Will I have to hand in my cleaning license if anyone ever looks in my corners 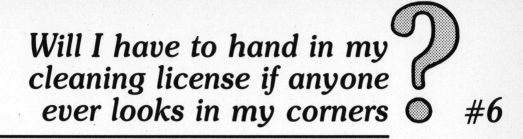 #6

WHITE GLOVE INSPECTION COMMITTEE

Shortly after the right angle was invented, some cleaning fanatic coined the phrase, "If you don't get the corners, it isn't clean!" So for centuries at home, in the office, and everywhere else we've worried about white-glove inspections of our corners—rather than the real problems: the centers.

The real reason we clean, aside from our sanitation concerns in certain places, is to remove dirt and grit and soil underfoot and in other friction areas before it damages and deteriorates furnishings, fixtures, and even the house itself. The occasional dead leaf or dust bunny that blows into the corner or lodges on the ledge threatens neither health nor home.

Yet I've watched fretting Freddies and frauleins on their hands and knees and in other awkward positions trying ceaselessly to keep the

13

corners clean. All you get is a sore back and prematurely aged cleaning equipment.

The corners and edges are actually what we pro cleaners call "nondepreciable areas"—which means they get almost no use or wear. So unless they're unsightly or Puppy's in-a-pinch potty place, they're really not hurting anything. Corner dirt is mostly emotional!

Look at your own house, for example—places like between the lamp and the armchair and out-of-the-way areas back against the wall. Some of these places are never set foot upon. They may see some minor action like a dropped magazine once a month or so—the rest of the time they just lie there.

But just three feet away the traffic patterns—like the area in front of the TV, couch, or stereo, the doorways and hallways and stairs—get thousands of trompings a month. Locations like in front of the sink and refrigerator, around the table, telephone, and trash cans get spills and scuffs and other assorted assaults, too. Yet we clean all of these areas with the same regularity, so we underclean the heavy use areas and overclean the corners.

We have a cobweb complex about corners, too. Cobwebs mean we're lousy cleaners; cobwebs let others know we haven't touched that spot in quite some time. But cobwebs can appear overnight. They do absolutely no damage except to passing gnats and can be whisked away in a second with a flick of a lambswool duster or broom.

Cutting corners will cut your cleaning time. Instead of the old equal attention to all areas, concentrate on the traffic patterns that deserve your diligence. It's not only logical—they're a lot easier to reach and clean than those corners and edges. Professional cleaners have been practicing this for years. Most cleaning crews in large buildings vacuum traffic patterns daily, other areas weekly, and corners and edges twice a month. If they can get away with it, so can you!

When you finally do have to do some corner cleaning don't try, as so many people do, to clean a square corner with a round or oversized tool—such as a mop, dust mop, regular broom, or upright vacuum. This approach just forces dirt into the corners and, in the case of wet mopping, causes little puddles of goop to collect there that eventually have to be scraped away. To prevent this, grab a few mop strands in your fingers and massage the corner as you pass. And you won't have wax buildup in the corners if you don't coat the corners every time you wax.

On a hard floor, an angle broom is best for edges and corners. On carpet, use your cannister vacuum. The crevice tool or the plain end of the wand, with no attachment at all, is the best way to empty a littered corner. You can also hit the corners and edges with a broom before you vacuum if you're using an upright vacuum or the pro cleaner's favorite approach—simply wipe the edges and corners with a damp cloth.

14

What's the best kind of scrub brush ❓ #7

A nylon pad! Scrub brushes are almost a thing of the past since the nylon mesh scrubbing pad came into the cleaning world. The reason is simple, as a quick self-experiment will show. Run a wet brush over the back of your hand, then a nylon scrub pad. The bristles of the brush look impressive, but once slanted backward as they usually are when you bear down on the brush and push it across a surface, their scrubbing action is as effective as the lash of a wet noodle. Try the same thing with a nylon scrub pad, and you'll feel the difference. It scrubs throughout the stroke. Twenty-five years ago all the scrubbing and polishing attachments on professional floor machines were natural fiber brushes, and they were a lot less effective than the nylon pads no pro cleaner would be caught without now.

My all-around favorite scrubbing tool, in fact, is a 3M Scotch-Bright #63 scrub sponge—yellow cellulose sponge on one side, white nylon scrub pad on the other. These won't damage even tender Tupperware or other plastics. You can use them to safely clean all kinds of easily scratched surfaces such as paint, plastic laminate (Formica), fiberglass, chrome and other plated metal, etc. The more aggressive green nylon pads can be used on floors, pots and pans, and tougher finishes. Be careful, though—all colored scrub pads are impregnated with abrasives that will scratch even metal and glass if you press too hard. The brown and black pads are the worst and should only be used on barbecue grills, concrete, or heavy wax buildup. Nyon scrub pads are available plain, without the sponge, too—but it's handy to be able to flip your scrubber over and have a wet sponge right in hand for wiping or a dry sponge for sopping up.

For floor scrubbing, the old hands-and-knees-with-brush routine has been happily rendered obsolete by another padded phenomenon—the long-handled swivel-head floor scrubber, the Doodlebug or Scrubbee Doo. You attach a pad of the right color to the Velcro-like pad holder on the head and scrub away. Your floor, shower stall, baseboard, siding, patio— and a hundred others—are not only scrubbed much better and faster but it's a lot easier on the back and knees.

You really do need a scrub brush to reach into deeply textured or indented or very irregular surfaces such as tile grout, grilles and slats, decking and siding, brick, and other rough masonry. The best kind to use is also the kind that will last the longest. A crimped nylon "utility brush"—just ask for that at the janitorial-supply store—is far easier to grip than the old classic scrub brush, and it keeps your knuckles well out of the nasties. It also reaches into corners better. A brush like this only costs about five dollars, and since the nylon handle and bristle bed don't absorb moisture, they won't rot or mildew or deteriorate. The nylon bristles hold up to the harshest chemicals and the hottest water, and they stay stiff when wet and in use, something the old brushes couldn't manage. They also don't frizz, shed, and flatten out as easily as natural bristles. And the whole brush is a cinch to clean, rinse, dry, and keep sanitary. Try one; you'll like it!

The only other scrub brush you probably won't want to do without is the one even professional cleaners haven't managed to replace—the old toothbrush. There's many a niche in the average house that only these will reach—so the only suggestion I have here is to always dip the end of the old toothbrush of the hour into bright fingernail polish, so nobody fails to realize it's the one you like to use to clean the crevice around the base of the toilet.

P.S. Your brushing technique is important, too. Instead of dragging the brush back and forth, hold it lightly against the surface and give it a gentle oscillating action. This keeps the ends of the bristles in constant contact with the surface you're trying to clean, scrubbing circles around each other.

What do you mean, "I" cause half of my own housework ? #8

THE "TOO MUCH" WE ALL HAVE TO DO.

200%

40% Junk & Clutter

50% Outdated & Inferior Tools & Techniques

30% Poor Design & Material Choice

20% Unrealistic Standards

15% Carelessness

10% Procrastination

35% Unavoidable Chores

That's wrong! You're actually personally responsible for at least three-quarters of your housework! Houses don't create housework—it's us, our families, our guests. And our bad habits.

1. Junk alone—you know, the old magazines and newspapers, unopened junk mail, empty containers, overstuffed garage, attic, basement, clothes closet, and all the rest—that we have in and around the house accounts for at least 40 percent of our housework time. When we aren't cleaning or dusting it, we're shifting and shuffling it around, sorting it, trying to find a place to put it, protecting it, or worrying about it. Yet a lot of this junk and clutter we never use and don't even really like. When

17

you toss it out, you toss an equal amount of cleaning time out with it! If it isn't there, it isn't in the way and doesn't have to be cleaned.

2. By the same principle, if no dirt gets in none has to be gathered up and gotten out. The American Carpet Institute says 80 percent of the dirt in our homes comes in from outside—on our feet. Good sense tells us that if we stop the dirt from getting in, we won't have to race all over the house sweeping and vacuuming and dustmopping and dusting it up. How do we stop it? By simply getting some professional-quality door-mats (see illustration).

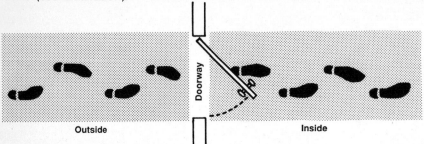

Outside   Doorway   Inside

Put a good set of "walkoff" mats at every entrance: rubber-backed synthetic turf outside, and nylon or olefin inside. Make sure they're at least four steps long on each side.

Hundreds of thousands of homemakers have discovered how to cut their cleaning time in half by using this and other **tools and techniques of the cleaning professionals.** The window cleaning that used to take four or five hours, for example, and end up streaky at that, now can be done spotlessly with a squeegee in thirty minutes. My first book, *Is There Life After Housework?*, is a short, painless course in taking the professional approach to every housekeeping chore. All you need is a little know-how and the right equipment—it's often less expensive than all the cleaning concoctions we cram into our cart at the supermarket.

3. Drudgery can be designed in or out. Did you ever stop to think that the colors you pick, the type of rugs, flooring, wall coverings, and furniture you buy, influence your cleaning time up to 50 percent? Whether you choose "pretty, but . . ." or practical can mean the difference between adding and substracting hundreds of hours of housework a year. For all the details of this you can look up a book my daughter and I wrote called *Make Your House Do the Housework.* **Where** in the house you allow predestined-mess behavior (eating, art and craft extravanganzas, roughhousing, pet guinea pig peregrinations) falls into this category, too.

4. Obsolete standards and overkill: does it really need to be done, or are you just in the habit of doing it? (See p. 74)

5. Don't procrastinate! Everything you don't handle right when it happens at least doubles your cleaning duty:

• A fresh spill can be taken care of in ten seconds. Try to clean it up later—after it's dried, hardened, soaked in, seeped down, spread, etc. —and you'll be at it at least ten or fifteen minutes (plus all the time you'll lose anguishing over the fact that the carpet or whatever now has a permanent spot or stain on it.

• The clothes you dropped right where you changed—you still have to spend the minute it would have taken to hang them up then, plus now the time to iron and delint them.

• It may take an extra five minutes now to put the garbage where the raccoons or the neighbor's ten-pound tom can't get to it. But that's much faster and more pleasant than collecting cracked chicken bones, ink-smeared papers, sticky boxes, oily cans, soggy Kleenex, and coffee-ground-filled orange halves all over the lawn and driveway. And then rebagging and rehauling it.

• Close it now and there's nothing to it—leave it open, and flies and mice get in, the prize animal gets out, heads get bumped, etc.

• Write it on the list—two seconds—get to the store, and try to recall what it was you needed—five minutes if you're lucky enough to remember at all, forty-five minutes if you have to make a second trip.

6. Not a little housework, too, is caused by **failure to think ahead or consider the consequences.** Laying down dropcloths or old newspapers or moving things out of the way before we start some splattery activity will never be particularly sexy—but a lot of sweeping, vacuuming, scraping, and refinishing would never be necessary if we only would.

Likewise, that extra Olympian—overvigorous—flair we like to put into everything from chopping cabbage to filling the water bucket to tossing our crumpled papers into the waste can usually means extra effort to pick up the overshot and overflowed.

Let's not forget what we do to ourselves, either, by setting things where they're sure to get knocked over or letting things boil over or burn.

Come to think of it, you may cause 85 percent of your own housework! Take it a little easier on yourself—starting today!

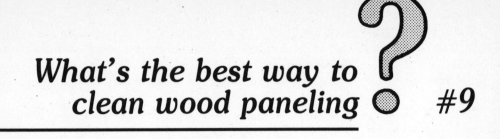

A good way to start is by making sure that it **is** real wood paneling. If the very same burls and swirls reappear every six feet or so on the wall, you no longer have to wonder whether it might be simulated wood. Paneling of this type is actually pictures of wood printed on plastic-coated paper mounted on masonite, plywood, or cheap pressboard. When cleaning this kind of "wood" paneling, you just want to wipe gently with a mild detergent solution. Never scrape or use steel wool or powdered cleanser on it, or you'll end up with some mismatched knot-holes in your pine pool room or fir covered family room.

If it does seem to be wood that you're dealing with, unless you have a very old house, it's unlikely to be solid planking. Wood paneling today is made of several thin layers of wood compressed or glued together,

20

cross-layered for strength, with a decorative wood veneer on the surface. The finished side almost always has several coats of urethane or varnish or a like protective coating applied to seal it off from intrusion of the household elements. But there is some paneling that's unsealed wood with only a coating of oil or wax over it. If it's an exotic expensive wood and you can feel the grain very clearly, assume that it is an oiled finish. And clean it only by reoiling it with tung oil or Danish oil or whatever was used on it last time, if possible. If it's wax that's on there now, rewax with a paste wax designed for wood and don't ever put oil on a waxed surface, or vice versa.

If what you've got is the much more common surface-sealed wood veneer paneling, you don't have to worry so much about the old warning to never use water on wood. When water or anything else hits this paneling, if the finish is intact, seldom does moisture get anywhere even close to the wood itself; all you're actually cleaning is the surface of the varnish or finish, which is fairly waterproof. You shouldn't baptize the wall, even so, but water used sparingly and wiped off quickly won't hurt. Water hurts wood only when it has time and space to soak in for a while; then it expands the grain of the wood and splits or rots it or loosens the binding glue and all that bad stuff. Professionals clean paneling just like they do walls; this is the right method:

• a bucket half-filled with a cleaning solution (in this case, a solution made with vegetable oil soap like Lin-Sol or Murphy's oil soap)
• an empty bucket
• a sponge
• a clean terrycloth cleaning cloth, folded in half

1) Dip the sponge only about half an inch into the solution (so it never gets so wet that water runs down the wall. 2) Start at the top of the wall and dampen about a three-by-three-foot area to dissolve the soil. Then go back over the wetted-down area with your sponge to pick up the soil and solution. 3) Dry and polish the sponged area with the cleaning cloth, working with the grain. 4) Always squeeze (don't twist) the dirty sponge into the empty bucket. Then dip the sponge into the clean solution again and do another section of the wall. 5) When you finish, the empty bucket will be full of dirty water, but your cleaning solution will stay crystal clear—so you know the chemical will always be working full strength for you.

On wood, you always want to use a mild vegetable oil soap or a neutral cleaner (which means it's not too alkaline or acid—just ask for a neutral cleaner at the janitorial-supply store) and apply the solution sparingly. If the surface is heavily soiled, make a stronger solution of the oil soap according to label directions and scrub the surface with a white nylon-backed scrub pad. You may also want to run over the surface with the upholstery brush of your vacuum before you start.

If you wipe with the grain when you're drying you'll never leave a streak. And the tiny bit of vegetable soap residue left behind when you're sponging will be buffed by your drying towel to a lovely low sheen. A clean, dry surface like this on a paneled wall is much better than covering the paneling with El Gunko panel polishes or lemon oils or expensive waxes that only build up on there and leave a sticky surface to collect and hold handprints and every passing particle of dirt and dust. And **oiling** a varnished or plastic-coated finish makes about as much sense as oiling glass. If your varnished wood walls have a polish buildup, clean with a degreaser or ammonia solution to cut the gunk, then apply the oil soap as described.

Remember that any raw, natural wood or unfinished paneling must be coated with a finish first before you wash it, so moisture won't penetrate the wood.

My husband's usual approach to cleaning is to "Armor All" everything—is that OK ❓ ● #10

How big is your husband? Products like Armor All, Clear Guard, and Beauty Seal aren't actually cleaners; they're coatings that seal, condition, and protect a surface. They do a good job of that and keep vinyl, for example, from getting hard, cracked, and brittle—but they should only be applied after the surface in question has been thoroughly cleaned. You could almost think of them as skin moisturizers rather than soaps.

Your question brings up a good point—we all have a tendency to think that if it shines it's clean. But even a filthy floor can shine if you put

23

something (such as a wax finish) on it that causes it to reflect light. Polishes that claim to "clean as they polish" are solidly in my suspicious column because of the inevitable question of where does the dirt go? Maybe it evaporates . . . doubtful. In with the coating, more likely.

Before you apply an Armor All-like product, clean the surface with the right kind of cleaner (vinyl cleaner for vinyl, saddle soap for leather, etc.). Once something is clean, Armor All–type products do just what their names imply, armor the surface with a slick coating of silicone that resists moisture, dust, and handprints. These products can be used to seal and protect just about any surface not harmed by water—vinyl car tops, dashboards, upholstery, chrome, sealed wood, rubber tires, fiberglass boats and shower stalls, finished leather, vinyl luggage, shoes, furniture, skis, etc. They dry to a clear, shiny surface that looks good and resists resoiling. They also contain a pentrating conditioner that softens and revitalizes vinyl and leather—deepens the color and helps protect against drying and fading. When applied to a clean surface, they reduce sun damage, oxidation, and tarnishing as well as slow the need for future cleaning and make it a lot easier to do when it must be done. A couple of cautions, though:

• Make sure the surface is not only clean but dry before applying the sealant (which means don't apply it in rain, dew, or 130 percent humidity).

• One coat may not be enough to do it—especially not on a very worn or weather-beaten finish.

• Use of these products on any painted surface makes repainting difficult (a silicone freak can make any painter paranoid), as it is next to impossible to get new paint to adhere to a slippery silicone-impregnated surface. Silicones will also make floors and steering wheels super slippery and put smears on glass that are maddeningly difficult to remove.

• Some of these products can also soften certain plastics and adhesives, so read the label and pay attention to what you're putting them on—don't just splash and spray away (even if the wet look is a little addictive). They're great for prolonging the life of vinyl tops on cars and other such uses, but they're not cure-alls or cleaners.

How can I get that burned-on stuff off the burner pans on the stove ? ○ #11

Ah yes, leave these babies for a few months and then try to get them clean, like my family and a few million others do. Whatever sloshes on the rings is tempered in place by heat and twenty more coats of whatever else boils over, and before you know it those things are as encrusted as the cannon of a sunken Spanish galleon.

There's a big hint of the answer to this question in the very term *burned-on*. When spills are allowed to dry out and burn on, they're at least ten times as hard to remove as when fresh. So part of the answer to this pesky problem is getting in the habit of wiping up stovetop spills

25

and spatters when they happen, while they're still wet and soft and spongeable. Then, too, you can apply the common sense rules of no-boilover cooking: don't start everything on high heat, use a pot or pan large enough to allow room for bubble-up and expansion, turn off the heat before you dash off to answer the phone or catch the cat, etc.

Since there may still be times when a spill or spatter can't be wiped up immediately, what else can you do to make those burned-on blotches easier to handle? First, line the reflector pans under the burners with aluminum foil. Then, instead of scrubbing and scouring them on cleanup day, you just quickly replace the foil. **Note:** I said "reflector pans," not "drip pans." Most people seem to think these little metal bowls are there specifically to catch spills, and they delight in covering them completely up with foil. But the real purpose of the pans is to reflect heat back up to the cooking surface, and the hole in the middle of the pan provides the air circulation essential for proper cooling. If you seal the hole shut, your electric burner elements will overheat and burn out long before their appointed hour. So be sure to leave any vent holes open, and smooth the foil out as much as you can over the pan—large crinkles can create damaging hot spots by focusing heat right back onto the element.

It's also a good idea to put a square of foil "down under," to cover the area under the burner where the gooey stuff goes when you have an all-out gourmet gusher. You don't want to leave layers of crusty strata down there that future archaeologists can use to trace your every cooking catastrophe. Again, be careful not to block any ventilation holes, especially on gas ranges. And don't try to line the whole "under cooktop area—just put a piece of foil directly under each burner to catch the drips that miss the lined reflector pan.

If you already have badly blackened cooktop pans and rings, here's the procedure for painless cleaning: Put the parts in a plastic tub filled with a strong hot solution of heavy-duty degreaser or dishwasher detergent and water and let 'em soak. (Don't use ammonia—it can darken aluminum.) Don't be in a hurry to start scrubbing—leave it all sit in the solution until those petrified puddles and fossilized overflows have really softened up. This may mean overnight, but it sure beats trying to scrub the stuff off before it's ready. It will help to pull out the pans from time to time and remove the already-softened layer so the solution can go to work on the hard stuff underneath. This can be safely and easily done with a white nylon-backed scrub sponge or a curly plastic Chore Boy.

If you have porcelain-coated reflector pans, they can go into the self-cleaning oven for easy cleanup when you run the oven through its cleaning cycle. Don't put chrome trim rings or aluminum parts or oven racks in there, though, unless you don't mind a darkened and stained look.

Don't use steel wool soap pads, green or brown or other colored nylon pads, or abrasive powdered cleansers on chrome burner pans unless you absolutely have to—they can scratch and mar the finish. Ditto in spades for Teflon coated pans. These more aggressive scrubbers can be used on the porcelain-covered burner grills on gas ranges and on aluminum reflector pans, unless they have a bright polished finish, in which case you should stick with a white nylon scrub sponge. In extreme cases, it may be necessary to gently scrape off hard deposits with an old butter knife, but be careful to wet the surface first and try not to scratch the finish. Avoid scraping and harsh scrubbing as much as you can, in general—let the soaking and the chemical action of the cleaning solution do the work.

Food deposits on the heating elements themselves can be burned off, but don't just turn it on high and let it smoke or you'll damage the element. Put a pan of water on to boil on high heat and turn on the hood fan. Let the water boil until any food fragments on the element are completely charred and have stopped smoking. Then after the element has cooled, the charred food can be scraped off gently with a dull knife and the element wiped down with hot, soapy water.

When should I change the washwater  #12

CLUNK!

Never . . . yes, never! If you're doing it right your washwater will be used up before it ever gets dirty. You clean with two buckets, one filled with cleaning solution—your washwater—and the other empty. When you wash a floor or wall and you finish your first pass with the sponge or mop, you always squeeze it into the empty bucket. Only then do you dip the sponge or mop back in to soak up the cleaning solution. Do it this way and your cleaning water will never get a drop of dirt in it. Use it until it's gone and make up a fresh bucket when and if you need it. When you're finished you just dump the second bucket (now partly filled with **really** dirty water). The two-bucket system can be used for floors, walls, woodwork, appliances, counters—about 96 percent of interior surface cleaning.

When you have no choice but to use the old dip-the-sponge-right-back-in-the-soup routine, keep your eye on the color of the solution. Don't just go by the number of dead bugs floating on top or the amount of grit and sludge in the bottom. When you can't see a quarter after you drop it in, it's time for a change. You'll be surprised how fast this rolls around. We don't always feel like making that extra trip back to the sink, so we get mighty good at convincing ourselves that we can actually **clean** something with **dirty** water!

Cleaning with a dirty solution doesn't just look bad and muddy our cleaning morale. It puts dirt right back on the surface, contaminating it and causing streaks and film and smudges. Once any cleaning solution gets dirty it loses its "power," and this is particularly true of disinfectants. A cleaning solution cleans by dissolving dirt and holding it suspended in the water, so you can dump it away down the drain. A certain amount of solution can only suspend so much dirt—after that it's just going to be spreading it around and redepositing it. At some point your bucket isn't a cleaning tool; it's just, as one pro cleaner put it, "a holding tank for dirty and disabled solution."

Which direction do you clean ? ⬤ #13

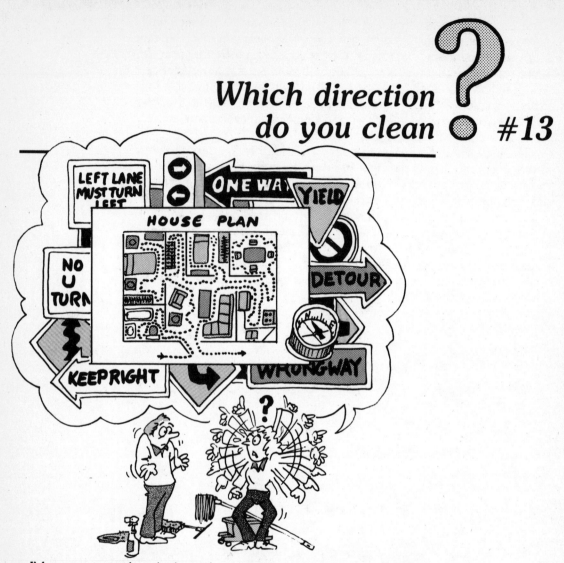

I'd never stopped to think just how important direction was in cleaning until a writer from *Family Circle* asked me, "Hey, Don, which direction to you clean—up and down, back and forth, or out the door?" I never clean out the door, and I hope you don't either—the only place you might want to consider that is in the barn.

Direction can make a big difference in your cleaning efficiency, and there are three right directions to go:

1. Top to bottom is only logical and most of us do take this approach, unless we've read and believed the old wive's tale about washing walls from the bottom up. You never want to do that. Years ago when the paints were calcimine and the cleaning solution almost pure lye soap, a drip from the top down would streak the wall, but not anymore. You want to work from the top down in all cleaning, so that gravity carries the dirty solution, dust particles, dead flies, etc., down the wall, woodwork, shelves, stairs, etc., ahead of you as you go. The dust and debris get knocked on the floor to be swept or vacuumed away. Then the floor that you tromp on and set buckets and cleaning equipment on is always the last thing you clean.

That means you do things like the tops of drapes first, too. There's lots of dust and airborne dirt up there, and running your duster across the top or taking them down for the cleaners **after** you've done the floor only means one thing—hauling out the broom or vacuum again!

2. Counter-clockwise (toward the sink and storage). Most right-handed people work faster if they move in a counter-clockwise pattern (from right to left) within a work area. Moving from room to room in a counter-clockwise direction, too, helps you keep track of where you've been and eliminates unnecessary steps. What we always want to avoid when it comes to cleaning is traipsing back over the clean area to change equipment, empty buckets, wring mops, and dump trash. Unless you're much steadier than most of us, you'll leave a mess. Ninety percent of the time when we do a big cleaning campaign we want to station ourselves in the kitchen and work from the farthest rooms back toward it. The kitchen is generally where our cleaning stuff is stored and where we get water, mix up cleaning solutions, etc., so if there are any spills or dropped litter here it'll all be in the area yet to be cleaned. I also get rid of any accumulated trash and clutter before I start on the kitchen or the last area, so that when I finish there I'm through!

3. North and south—east and west. When it comes to the actual hands-on cleaning, the direction you go is important, too. Most of us just make a circular swabbing motion or an enthusiastic back and forth attack. Neither of these does a complete job on any surface. Think of it—even a carpet that lies flat on the floor is composed of individual fibers that stand up and each carpet strand actually has four sides to clean. If you go back and forth, you clean two sides, which is better than nothing, but it doesn't do it all.

From now on, when you're cleaning, approach it like a dance pattern. Whether you're sweeping, shampooing, or scrubbing, give it the old samba step—go north and south (up and down) first, then east and west (back and forth). Repeat this maneuver in smooth, even strokes and observe the difference, as you get the dirt out from all surfaces on all sides. Going first in one direction, then back over the same area in the opposite direction is good practice, whether you're washing walls, mowing grass, painting, or applying fertilizer. An overlapping, crisscross pattern assures a first-class job—smooth, even coverage and no missed places.

Why does my vacuum seem to pick up so poorly these days ? #14

WHiRRRRRRRRRRRRR!!

You remember the demo day, when your vacuum was new and the salesman could barely tear the hose off his hand. Today it still sounds the same and looks the same, but you have to pick up the popcorn hulls by hand while your vac provides the sound effects!

Your vacuum is probably still in good general health, but a few little things may have been wounded somewhere along the carpet trail.

The bag. Cloth bags should pass air and hold dust. In time they pass dust and hold air because of leaks and clogging of the bag's pores with dust. If it's leaking, replace it. If clogged, shake it vigorously over a newspaper or turn inside out and vacuum it thoroughly with a canister vac. (Some people even wash them in the clothes washer.) Replace disposable bags (see p. 101) before they're anywhere near full. If you have a canister vac, clean or replace the motor filter, too.

The beater bar. This little revolving unit near the front of an upright or in the power wand of a canister has the biggest job to do. It beats and combs and "bounces" the carpet, to dislodge dirt and debris so the suction can pull it up into the bag. If the bristles on the bar are worn down the beater can't do its job and you're stuck with suction alone. Likewise, a stretched belt, or a belt slipped off its pulley or on backward will cut the best beater bar's efficiency up to 50 percent. Or look down under the vacuum (when its **off**) and you may see strings and strands of whatever you ran too close to wrapped as tightly as a tourniquet around the bar and its brushes, slowing it down.

Pile height adjustment can also affect the bar's ability to do its thing. The height should be set so that the brushes just flick the top of the carpet as they pass over it. If you hear the motor "pull down" when the vacuum is set on the carpet, the brushes are set too low.

Plugged hose. A canister vac every once in a while gets a pin, toothpick, or broom straw hung up in the hose and it catches furballs and fuzz and everything imaginable and restricts air passage. Run a long, thin pole or a garden hose (dry, of course) through it, and before you know it the patient will be breathing normally.

The impeller. The spinning impeller or fan is what gives a vacuum its suction. In canisters the impeller is protected by a filter, but in uprights whatever you vacuum up goes right through the fan. Over time, the tacks, coins, BB's, buttons, paper clips, nails, and little rocks even the carefullest cleaner picks up will chip and chisel away the blades of the fan and cut your suction way down. A new impeller only costs about five dollars, and you can install it yourself or have a repair shop do it.

Vacuum shops all over have checkup specials for twenty-five dollars or so. You can take your faithful servant in for a physical, replace a few parts, and it'll be as good as new. I've seen vacuum motors and cases that have lasted for half a century; yours can do it, too. I know lots of people who, instead of buying a new machine for three hundred dollars, pick up a used one for fifteen to twenty dollars, replace the bag, impeller, and beater bar, and have themselves a perfectly good vacuum!

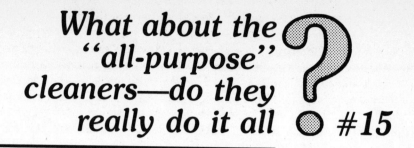

Think of it like sandpaper. The hardware store has more than twenty grades, from gravel coarseness to smooth as slate. In that whole range from 00 to 600 grit, there's one that would be ideal for each sanding situation we come up against. But I don't want twenty-odd abrasive papers on my workbench. So I keep one fine, one medium, and one coarse sandpaper on hand, and they work fairly well for the majority of my sanding projects.

34

Likewise, no one soap or detergent can do a perfect job on all sorts of soils and surfaces. Almost any chore we tackle a specialty cleaner will do better than an all-purpose potion. Manufacturer's claims notwithstanding, no one cleaner can do it all. A detergent designed to work on laundry will leave spots and streaks if used on dishes or windows. Liquid dishwashing detergent, made to be mild to the hands, isn't powerful enough to use in the automatic dishwasher and would flood the floor with suds if we did. Each cleaner is formulated with a particular purpose in mind, and there indeed are limits to how "all-purpose" any one cleaner can get. But if you don't want a whole smorgasbord of specialty products bulging out from under your sink, you can choose a few broad-range cleaners that can handle most everyday household operations.

First of all, forget about the home brews so dear to the heart of the hint and tip columnists and old wives' tale collectors. Most of these are concocted with natural soaps and phosphates such as TSP, washing soda, soap flakes, borax, etc. There are good reasons why these old standbys were replaced by modern synthetic detergents; namely, phosphates are damaging to the environment and natural soaps don't work well in cold water or hard water. Forget saving a few pennies by mixing your own cleaners out of ingredients from Grandma's day—buy good modern cleaners that take advantage of what we've learned since then.

What do you want in your basic cleaning arsenal? For starters, you never want to use any stronger a cleaner than necessary to get the job done. Most "all-purpose" cleaners sold on the supermarket shelves should really be labeled "heavy-duty" cleaners. Most of them are much too strong for simple chores like mopping the kitchen floor. Cleaners like these will soften and remove floor finish ("wax") and often leave a detergent film that dulls the shine.

For jobs calling for a mild cleaner, such as floor mopping, general spot cleaning, wiping down vinyl, or washing the car, I'd use a neutral cleaner from a janitorial-supply store or just a liquid dish soap like Joy. And don't use too much of it—it only takes a little squirt of Joy, for example, in a mop bucket to do a good job on floors, ten drops or less for squeegeeing windows. Hand dish detergents are extra sudsy, so if you overdo it, you'll be there forever rinsing them away.

An alcohol-based spray window cleaner (such as Windex or the janitorial-store equivalent) is also a handy cleaner to have around as we've all discovered. It makes fast work of small windows, mirrors, chrome, appliances, and countertops. You can use it on just about any synthetic surface where you want a streak-free shine—but never on raw wood or other porous finishes.

You'll still want one of the more powerful "all-purpose" cleaners and degreasers in the closet, but reserve it for really stubborn spot cleaning, such as removing crayon and lipstick marks, hardened cooking spills, grease removal, and like tough assignments. Many of these products can damage paint and household metals if used straight or left on too long, so read the label, don't forget to rinse, and don't go wild with them.

Another product I always like to have on hand is a disinfectant cleaner. A quaternary disinfectant (see p. 123) is great for cleaning, sanitizing, and deodorizing any surface where bacteria growth and odors are a problem—bathroom fixtures, diaper pails, garbage cans, sickrooms, etc. Or you can use a pine cleaner with at least 20 percent pine oil, such as Pine Power or Pine-Sol and it will double as a deodorizing disinfectant and heavy-duty cleaner.

These few preparations, plus your laundry room regulars and a few specialized polishes, should take care of all your cleaning needs. If the chemists keep working on it, they might just come up with an all-purpose cleaner—capable of almost any cleaning assignment, and yet safe for humans and all home surfaces. For the time being, though, we'll have to keep several different products on hand, along with our several grades of sandpaper.

Do I really need to take everything up and off the floor when I strip or wax it ⬤ #16

The rugs, mats, dog, kids, and bedroom slippers should always be moved before any floor cleaning job. If you're just going to wet mop, that's all I'd move. If you're going to really clean it up, do a little scrubbing and rewax the traffic areas, I'd take the table and chairs, the high chair, the trash receptacles, and anything light enough to lift and set it out of the room—no sense in cleaning, mopping, and waxing (that's three times) around and under objects that can be moved. And who wants to wax things to the floor?

If you're doing a full-fledged stripping job, that once every eighteen months marathon, I'd move everything movable except perhaps the loaded china closet, the stove, and the fridge (unless you can't resist

37

seeing what's under there). In general, leave it in place if it would be harder to move it than to work around it.

The things you don't move at least dust mop under if you can, and be careful not to let rivers of stripping water flow under them. True, the floor under there isn't being used and can't be seen, but if you let the solution puddle under there it can be caustic enough, once the water evaporates away, to damage and dull the surface of your tile or linoleum. It may also cause the metal bottoms, feet, and coasters of things to rust and stain the floor. File cabinets are famous for creating rust lines during the stripping process, and those stains aren't easy to get out!

If you're determined to at least "do behind there," move it out, strip behind it, let it dry, and put it back. You only want to wax up to it where it'll be when it's in place—not under it.

When moving big, heavy things like appliances be careful not to tear the flooring. Cushioned vinyl, especially, wounds easily. If you put a throw rug or a thick towel under the front feet and then pull on it, the appliance should slide right out.

When the moment rolls around for moving things back, even though the wax seems dry in twenty minutes, let it have an hour or so to really cure and get good and hard before you haul all that stuff back onto it. Shuffling furniture around on it while it's still soft will scratch and mar that sparkling new surface.

Is a rag or a sponge better to clean with **?** ● #17

Calling a cleaning cloth a "rag" is really uncouth—I don't want to hear you do that again. It gives cleaning a bad image!

I'll give the sponge the decision in the first round, for washing and scrubbing. Sponges are easier to hold and handle—they can even be cut to fit any size hand. They hold five times the liquid a cloth does and distribute it over the area you're trying to clean ten times as well (as in faster and more evenly, especially on large, flat surfaces). A sponge will sop up big liquid spills more speedily and less drippily than a cloth, and a sponge is easier to rinse and refill with solution. Sponges don't get rank and smelly as fast as rags do either, probably because a certain self cleaning action comes into play every time we squeeze them.

Before we consider the virtues of cloths, let's make it clear that the only kind you should consider letting into your cleaning cabinet is cotton

39

terry toweling. A nice big, thick, thirsty piece of terry toweling will give you a supply of professional-quality cleaning cloths that can't be beat for absorbing and polishing (see pg. 176 for instructions on how to make them). Those old polyester pants, permanent-press shirts, and semitransparent sheets that work their way into the "ragbag" absorb water poorly or not at all, and those leftover buttons, zippers, collars, ruffles, cuffs, and hems don't help much, either. Cleaning cloths are at their best in buffing things dry. If you get them wet enough to really apply a solution, they drip and flood down your arm. They should really be partners—the sponge for applying and swabbing and the cloth for wiping dry and polishing. If you're cleaning a little part of something or polishing a window or mirror or a piece of chrome, etc., a cloth and a spray bottle is fine, but if you're doing heavy cleaning, use the sponge to apply your solution and a cloth to dry and shine.

You can exert more fingerpower with a cloth, so they are usually superior for spot cleaning, as well as in situations where it's important to be able to come up with a lot of clean sides without walking back to the bucket. And nothing can reach tight places or all the contours of little objects like knickknacks and figurines as well as a damp cloth.

If you don't want to shorten their life span, don't leave sponges and cleaning towels out in the sun or bleach them. What sense does it make to try to get a cleaning tool snowy white anyway? Don't use fabric softener when you launder your cleaning cloths, or you'll put a film on them that interferes with their function. Remember, too, that you wring your hands, or a chicken neck, but never your faithful servant the sponge—just **squeeze** it. And if a surface is jaggy enough to snag your rag or trap tiny pieces of sponge everywhere you ought to be using a brush on it!

When you go to get yourself a sponge, you don't want the shiny close-grained "plastic" or polyester kind—have you ever tried to get one to absorb water? About the only thing they're good for is car cleaning or working with acid cleaners, to which they'll hold up much better than a cellulose sponge. For ordinary cleaning, use a cellulose sponge or, if you'll be doing a lot of scrubbing with it, a nylon-backed cellulose sponge. If you're feeling flush and have access to them—you might even consider a natural sea sponge. Window washers still swear by them, because they last longer and hold an amazing amount of water. Plus they're just plain a pleasure to close your hand around.

Is there some smart way to clean convoluted surfaces like heavily carved woodwork ? ● #18

Pretty too often means fluted, grooved, scrolled, curlicued, carved, curved, notched, niched, sculpted, or deeply indented—all ideal ways to collect dirt and dust buildup. No wonder old woodwork, etc., often looks gummy. Stuff like this is about as tough to clean as it was to produce— lots of hand work! Doing any of this one crack or groove at a time will put you into the rubber room.

The first mystery to solve here is—can you use water on it? Any

41

ornate woodwork or trim should be painted with a good semigloss enamel or clear urethane so that you can use generous amounts of water on it without worrying. A water-based cleaning solution is what we really need to deal with deep relief or heavy contour or elaborate detail. Water can go where no tool can reach, into all the little areas where dirt has hidden, and dislodge and dissolve it and float it away. You just have to make sure you get the water on and off anything wooden as quickly as possible—you don't ever want to let even well-sealed wood "soak" more than a few minutes. If the object is dusty, dust it with a soft paintbrush or vacuum dust-brush attachment first to avoid making mud when you pour the water on.

A flexible bristled nylon scrub brush is a big help here. Sponge the solution (vegetable oil soap solution, for wood) onto the surface, then give it a minute or two to work before giving it a thorough brushing. The brushing technique you want here is very much like the way you use a toothbrush to massage your gums. Don't drag the brush back and forth—hold it lightly against the surface and agitate the tips of the bristles into the crevices and indentations. Black foam will usually emerge, which you can wipe away with a dry towel. Remember, though, that even if you loosen it with scrubbing and chemical action, dirt and soap can remain deep in the cracks and crannies, so you have to do more than wipe the surface when you're rinsing to remove it. I always find a way to flood-rinse or douse the surface so all the residue can run out and off. If necessary, protect surrounding surfaces with thick towels when you do this. If the surface you're cleaning is really dirty, you may need to repeat the process. Just bear in mind that the right kind of scrubbing and **ample water** is the secret. Then remove the remaining moisture by blotting and pressing with a thick, clean towel.

Small waterproof objects are best washed in the sink or bathtub where you can use lots of rinse water and maybe the sink spray head. For attached items like woodwork you just have to sponge the water on liberally and have plenty of towels on hand to soak up the runoff. If the dirt is solidly entrenched and the surface can stand it, a stronger solution, firmer brush, or even a pressure washer will often do the trick. For anything water-resistant you can take outside a good blasting out with a garden hose nozzle will often work wonders.

How can I ever get around to the deep cleaning ? ○ #19

All I ever have time to do is "surface clean" or straighten up.

Deep cleaning is all those things that "ought" to be done, but they don't have to be done this minute. They **could** wait, and as our lives get busier and busier they do wait. We don't have weeks and often not even whole weekends to devote to deep cleaning anymore, so how **do** we manage to get it done?

Do a little every week/day. One sure way to reduce the deep cleaning in the future is to increase your daily surface cleaning just a little—say 5 percent. Things that are kept clean seldom need deep cleaning! "Cleaning as you go"—every day, all year round—can nearly eliminate deep cleaning entirely. So sneak some little deep cleaning chore into every cleaning session: clean out one cupboard or one drawer; dust do all the high dusting; wash one set of curtains or one shelf of dusty goblets in the china closet. You don't have to pick it out ahead of time—in fact, it helps to give yourself free rein here. But don't make it too ambitious, so it stays scarcely noticeable and doesn't derail your general cleaning agenda for the day. There are only so many corners and surfaces in a house, and if you keep chipping away at it you **will** make a dent.

Don't fail to act when the impulse strikes. Deep cleaning energy is too rare, too fine, too exotic to ever be wasted. If the urge suddenly comes over you to dejunk the bulletin board, ditch all the outdated seed catalogs, sweep the unspeakable cellar, or finally face up to the inside of the storage shed or refrigerator, don't let anything short of salaried employment or deathbed pledges get in your way. And if you get started and have a genuine desire to keep going, take the half-day of vacation you still have coming or postpone lunch with Aunt Lottie and keep on going.

Snatch those sudden bonazas when the company can't make it, the concert is canceled, or your Ping-Pong match is postponed; we're so overscheduled these days we never have "free" time unless it was originally allotted to something else. You've finally got it—don't waste it!

Plan a deep cleaning expedition for sometime when you **do** have a stretch of time—such as a long weekend in honor of a holiday you've never given a hoot about and your beloved will be at the bass finals anyway. Recreation, after all, is a pretty relative thing—once we're over thirty we realize **anything** we want to do badly counts—and that even includes deep cleaning. Deep cleaning (the under, over, inside, behind, and ignored portions of a house) can almost be fun once we actually get into it. Regular daily surface cleaning is the same old thing every day—here we get a chance to explore some forgotten region of our house!

Do it first especially if it's only one thing on your list of to dos for the day. Deep cleaning does take extra emotional and physical energy, so go to it before the sap evaporates or the adrenaline runs out.

Start with a garage sale, a great incentive for deep cleaning. Once you dejunk, your all-out once a year attack on the house will be half done!

Corner yourself with commitment such as inviting someone you're in awe of to come stay for a weekend.

Divide it up. The pros can clean carpet, for example, faster, easier, and cheaper than you can, so let them do it. Call and schedule a carpet cleaning, it'll force you, again, to finish the cleaning before the carpet guys come.

Do it by degrees if you must. Even the biggest job can be broken into steps or layers that can be tackled one by one. You can even clean a closet or an oven in stages if you have to. Even if you don't get as far

44

as you'd planned by a given point, don't get discouraged or give up. If you keep on making progress you'll make it.

Don't try to do too much. Don't predoom your deep cleaning project by running it head on with some other intensive activity. And don't bite off too big a piece for the time you have available.

Don't get deflected. There's undone deep cleaning on every side, so no matter how littered the garage suddenly looks or how badly the ceiling fan blades beg to be dusted, stick with getting the bugs out of the light fixtures. Otherwise you'll have six things started and nothing really finished and end up down on deep cleaning.

And before you even start that chore, **are you sure you need to do it?** (See p. 74)

Do dust ruffles serve any real purpose ? #20

It's hard for me to find a polite answer to that because thirty years of professional cleaning in hundreds and thousands of homes I've had to dodge around dust ruffles while trying to clean around and under beds and shampoo couches and chairs. They get butted by the dust mop and sucked up in the vacuum, and they're the delight of cats and kittens—so they catch, snag, shred, stain, and fray. There are a million and one grimies that can land on a dust ruffle, even if your kids don't watch Saturday morning cartoons eating cereal in your bed. And then to clean it after Rover's marked it and your husband's dirty boots have been parked on it you have to heave-ho the mattress, wash and dry the thing, run around the bed several times to reposition it properly again, reheave

46

and replace the mattress, then hope that the wrinkles hang out of it. Or even if you got the kind that tacks on with upholstery pins, it may take a dozen rounds to have it on there proper. That's a lot of effort to hide a box of sweaters. Worst of all, dust ruffles harbor and encourage fuzz balls; they don't prevent them. Unless you like to lose things under your furniture for weeks or months at a time, I'd do without dust ruffles. It makes more sense to keep the area under furniture open and accessible for easy cleaning than to try to hide what we know is collecting there.

How can I keep my guests from causing me a lot of extra work after they leave ❓ ⬤ #21

There's no doubt that a lot of the messes we clean up aren't ours but those left by relatives, friends, neighbors, and others. We love to have people come by, and most visitors leave a good feeling, but many also unthinkingly leave a mess, too. Crumbs and spills, dirty dishes, crumpled napkins and candy wrappers, cigarette butts, photos and magazines and records and towels strewn about, toys left out—the list goes on and on. When all this is left for one or two people to clean up, it's a big job and can even erode the afterglow of a pleasant visit.

A lot can be done to change this, and it's mainly a matter of training your guests. If you act like you don't care, others (even ordinarily neat people) simply won't worry about leaving a mess. If you give them some gentle hints that you expect them to pick up after themselves and make it easy for them to do so, most people will cooperate, and that even includes grandkids. They may even enjoy the visit more as a result—doing is always more fun than just sitting, and you can always **talk** while doing. Then too, many people actually feel uncomfortable (a little guilty) if they don't help out—so you'll be relieving them of such sensations, too.

A little bit of example goes a long way here. When you get up from the table, scrape and rinse your own plate and load it into the dishwasher; your guests will get the cue to follow suit. Travelers are always in need of laundry services, so it's nice to say at bedtime, "There's detergent and fabric softener in the laundry room if you have some things you'd like to throw in, so help yourself." You could even add, "Stick the towels in if you need to fill out a load." My mother-in-law even sets out sheets on the day of departure for her guests to switch on the bed—she's got the right idea, and you know, people love to come to her house and think she's the most gracious of hostesses.

When someone offers to help, take him or her up on it. Don't just blurt out "Oh, don't bother," "I'll get it," or "Don't worry about that, you just sit down and enjoy yourself." Most visitors (and especially those staying for a while) would feel better if they could clean up after themselves. But we too often, in our eagerness to wait on and "host" our guests, eliminate their opportunity. Don't do it. When visitors volunteer to do the dishes or make the bed or help straighten up before they leave, *let them!*

Come right out and ask for help if necessary once or twice and you'll **get** it—and you won't have to ask next time. After a meal you can just say, "Who'd like to rinse [load? wipe the table?] while I clear the leftovers." After all, everyone cheerfully clears off their own table at McDonald's, because it's expected. People love to help and if you ask in a good-natured way and express some real thanks when they're through, you'll always get more help than you ask for.

"Not knowing where anything goes" is always a big hindrance to the helping process. So make sure it's easy to see where to put the trash, trays, toys, etc. Have a rack or other clearly designated area for reading materials and wastebaskets out in plain sight so guests know where to put things.

Bring out some mess savers **before** guests arrive: a stack of paper cups at every faucet; a tall trash can with liner in a conspicuous corner of the kitchen—it won't crimp your decor just this once (and spare bags in the bottom, under the liner); an extra roll of paper towels on the counter—maybe one in the bathroom too; and if there are toddlers, boxes of wet-wipes upstairs and down, not only for sticky fingers, but to clean the TV knobs and tabletops that sticky fingers touch.

Have a maid caddy or shelf of cleaning supplies and tools handy, and let guests know where it is. Ordinary cleanup aside, there'll always be spills and accidents, nosebleeds, cut fingers, and maybe even a wee bit of upchuck on the carpet. Most people will be grateful for the opportunity to clean up their own messes, if you have the supplies handy for them. This includes a spray bottle of all-purpose cleaning solution and some cleaning cloths and a simple carpet spotting kit for quick removal of spots and stains. Put a scrub sponge on the edge of the tub and the sink and let them know where the broom and dustpan, vacuum, and laundry baskets are kept.

P.S. Be sure to let family and friends know that you *do* appreciate them pitching in before they leave. A wonderful side benefit from all this is that you'll enjoy having company—visitors, family—more than ever, and you can't beat that!

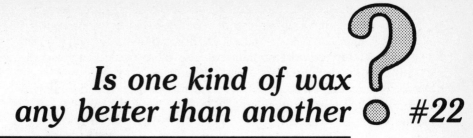

Is one kind of wax any better than another ? ● *#22*

First off, it really isn't wax anymore, unless you're talking about the special solvent or paste waxes made for wood or cork floors. We used to polish our floors with naturally occurring waxes like carnauba, but today we use modern polymer (plastic) floor finishes almost everywhere. We still tend to speak of this as "wax" and "waxing," however, even though the true wax products are about all gone. Paste waxing is just too tedious and time consuming for most of us. Even a wood or cork floor I'd seal with several good coats of urethane and forget about waxing it.

You undoubtedly asked this question because other people's floors always seem a lot shiner than yours. They probably aren't; it just seems that way because we look at our own floor a lot more often, under all kinds of conditions. There's something else to bear in mind here about this business of shining floors. It's not usually the wax or finish's fault that the floor doesn't shine—if a floor is old and worn and dull or rough, even cleaning and waxing it with several coats won't produce a gloss finish. A floor with a new or undamaged surface, on the other hand, can often be buffed up to shine like the sun, even when no finish at all has been applied.

What about those beautiful floors you see in places like malls and supermarkets that look as if there's a sheet of glass right over the floor—and with all that traffic on them, too! We professional cleaners call this the "wet look," and we get it by using a thermoplastic floor finish and a high speed burnisher. Heat from the friction of the burnishing pad softens the finish and smooths it out and polishes it to a shine you can see your face in. Most homemakers don't want to buy an eight-hundred-dollar machine and buff their floors daily even to get this kind of shine, so a self-polishing (no buff) finish is what most of us need.

You apply wax or finish to a floor for three basic reasons:

1. For protection: floor finish forms a protective layer that keeps damaging grit and soil particles away from the tile or vinyl or linoleum itself so they can't scratch and abrade the surface and wear it out.

2. To enhance appearance: floors are the number one thing noticed, and if they're clean and shining, people love it and it makes you feel good.

3. To aid cleaning: waxed floors are much easier to clean because the soil and black marks are on the wax, not on and embedded in the floor itself.

Vinyl composition tile, sheet vinyl, and linoleum are porous and must be sealed and protected with floor finish. Even the so-called no-wax floors will eventually need a finish on them to protect and beautify, although many people prefer to leave them waxless until they start to dull out. No-wax floors have a clear layer of polyurethane or vinyl on top that acts like a thick built-in coat of wax. If you keep the floor clean of damaging grit, this factory-installed shine should last a long time. Eventually, though, scratches and wear will dull the gloss in the traffic areas and you'll have to apply a finish if you want an even shine.

So which wax should you go for? Of the supermarket products, Mop and Glo and Future are both good, if you take the trouble, catchy names notwithstanding, to clean the floor first. But the best deal will be found on the shelves of your janitorial-supply store. Ask them for their best commercial nonyellowing self-polishing floor finish, such as Johnson's Complete or Top Gloss. Buy their top-of-the-line product, and you'll get a finish that will wear better than the supermarket brands and most likely cost less, too. If you apply a couple of coats of a finish like this it should last for months; just don't clean the floor with a strong alkaline cleaner, like ammonia or Spic and Span, that will soften the wax and cause it to look cloudy. And don't use too much of any detergent—this not only deshines the surface, but leaves a soap film that dulls the appearance of the entire floor. A healthy squirt of dish detergent or one quarter-cup of neutral cleaner in a couple gallons of warm water is all you need for mopping and daily maintenance of resilient floors, whether they have finish on them or not.

What is dust, anyway—does it actually harm anything 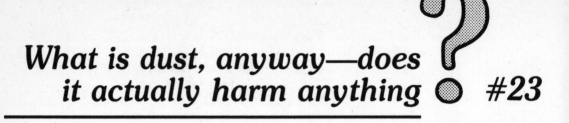 *#23*

There are at least five thousand possible ingredients in dust, and the average house accumulates forty pounds of it a year! That can be a little discouraging, since we seem to have adopted dust as the general indicator of household cleanliness. At least 50 million tons of dust settle on U.S. surfaces a year, and it costs businesses about six hundred dollars a pound to have it expunged from their premises.

That fine, fluffy layer lounging on everything we own is composed of tiny particles of rock, topsoil, sand, sawdust, salt from the oceans, carbon from smoke, ash from comets and volcanos, fibers from our clothing, carpets, drapes, furniture, bedding, and teddy bears, skin flakes, mold spores, pollen, bits of plants, insects, and pet and human hair. You really don't want to know the other 4,981 ingredients, do you?

Innocent-looking as it is, dust actually does more than ruin our housekeeping reputation:

• The tiny spores snuggled into dust spread bacteria and virus infections.

• Quite a few of us are allergic to dust or more precisely to the microscopic dust mites that inhabit it—so dust is responsible for a lot of sneezing, coughing, headaches, and runny noses.

• Dust in the air and on all our household surfaces from refrigerator tops to recliner cushions combines with airborne grease to form a sticky film that gums up everything and is hard to get off.

• Small as they may be, dust grains are abrasive (there's rock and soil and sand in there, remember?), and over time they'll destroy carpet fibers and floor finishes especially.

• Dust cuts the efficiency of many of our household machines and interferes with the operation of electronic equipment from stereos to personal computers.

• Dust clogs the pores of our houseplants and the coils of our refrigerator.

• Dust can even be a fire hazard and a place for people to write things we don't want to read!

So dust does a lot, over time, to depreciate your home and its contents and, to demoralize, you too! What do we do about it?

For one thing, many of our dusting methods should really be labeled "dust distribution practices," as we use dust flingers to clean with instead of dust collectors. Think about it—when you use a feather duster, where does the dust go? It's just redistributed around. Using brooms and rags, etc., may get the bulk of it, but never all the fine stuff, which just gets blown all over every time there's an air current, from a ventilation fan or a passing person. What do we professionals do? We keep it out—and what does get in we capture. I've seen homes and commercial buildings treated this way go for two weeks untouched and almost zero dust accumulates—that's our goal. And it costs so little to accomplish.

First **prevent.** 1. Make sure you have good mats at all entrances—inside and out (see p. 18). 2. and a good filter system—which means clean, operating filters in your furnace and air conditioners—and you might even want to invest in some room air cleaners for problem areas or, better yet, a "precipitron" or electrostatic air cleaner for your central heating or cooling system. 3. Seal all dust-generating unfinished concrete floor surfaces with penetrating concrete seal. 4. See that soot-producing oil stoves and fireplaces are well vented. 5. Caulk, seal, or weatherstrip as necessary to help keep outside dust outside.

Second, **capture.** 1. Dust mop rather than sweep (see p. 63). 2. Make sure your vacuum bag isn't so full or dust-clogged that it's forcing as much dust out as it's taking in and keep the bag clip tight. A central vacuum (or even a water-circulating vacuum, if dust is a real health hazard for you) puts much less dust into the air than our conventional vacuums do. 3. Use the right kind of collecting tools. This means a lambswool duster for high areas and big stuff like beams and ceilings and the right kind of dust cloth. That doesn't mean a soft (usually dirty and linty) rag, but a professional's disposable dust cloth like the Masslinn, which is treated with a chemical that enables it to attract and hold even the finest dust. Or the cloth called New Pig that grips dust by electrostatic action and can be rewashed and reused up to a hundred times. (It's only available in beauty salons, and you can find out which ones by calling 1-800-822-3878.)

P.S. Don't think that dust is utterly devoid of merit. It's dust in the air that gives us those colorful sunsets, and as one homemaker put it, "I love my dust; it protects my furniture from the elements. And it marks the spot so I can put things back where they belong when I move them."

HELP! The floor drain in my laundry room stinks!—what should I do ? #24

Drains get stale when they're not used, just like anything else. Under that drain is a crooked pipe called a P trap. It's designed to trap the tail end of the water you flush down the drain and hold it there to seal off the opening so that the smelly gasses from the sewer or septic tank below can't feed back into your home. If you leave a drain unused long enough, the water in the trap will evaporate and with the obstruction gone that sewer gas will funnel right into the house. The trapped water (often dirty) will also stagnate and smell if left for any length of time. If you only use a drain once in a great while, the water in the trap isn't always being replaced by new water, as it is when you use a drain regularly. You can solve this problem easily by pouring a gallon of clean water down there about every two weeks. I always drop a little disinfectant cleaner in the water for added insurance.

P.S. There's an outside chance that your drain smells bad because a trap was never installed under it or the trap that's there is cracked or otherwise damaged. If the above course of action doesn't take care of it, have a plumber check it out.

Will soft water soften my cleaning chores ❓ *#25*

It doesn't take much hydro-homework to come up with a resounding "Yes!"

Soft water:

1. Can save more than half of the money you spend on soaps, detergents, and shampoo.

2. And it can save up to 50 percent of the time and energy you spend cleaning.

3. It reduces scaling that clogs your pipes and slows your drains.

4. It reduces toilet and tub ring, soap scum buildup, and staining of tubs, sinks, and showers.

58

5. It helps clothes, linens, plumbing, cooking utensils, and appliances last longer (up to twice as long!).

6. It eliminates the need for abrasives, acids, and bleaches that destroy surfaces.

7. It gives you softer and whiter clothes, shinier hair, and smoother skin!

8. It even saves you some on your energy bill.

Eighty-five percent of U.S. homes have hard water to some degree. Hardness is simply caused by invisible dissolved minerals in the water, mostly calcium and magnesium. This liquid "rock" keeps soap from lathering and even combines with soap to form a curd that leaves scummy deposits on laundry and sinks and tubs. It also leaves little cloudy mineral spots and ridges on everything from windows to hubcaps to shower heads.

Soft water cleans everything better, faster, and cheaper, no guessing about it. Dull gray or yellowed clothing, lusterless floors, spotted glassware, and crusty bathroom fixtures magically disappear when soft water moves in.

Soft water will not only save on cleaning aids such as soaps and detergents; it will cut your cleaning **time** down dramatically (no more fighting hard-water scale on faucets, shower stalls, and windows). And if you've ever had to replace an electric water heater element because of lime scale burnout, you know how much it can save you on appliance repairs.

You can soften water for your bath or for doing laundry with packaged (powdered) water conditioners, but that doesn't do anything for your poor old water heater, pipes, or bathroom fixtures. For an unlimited supply of soft water you need a machine, a water conditioner, that removes the calcium, magnesium, and iron by a process of ion exchange. You can rent, lease, or buy modern water conditioning equipment that operates automatically and requires very little maintenance. Your local soft water appliance dealer will be happy to test your water and tell you all you need to know.

If you're on a low-sodium diet, you may want to consider additional filtering equipment for your cooking/drinking water, since the ion exchange process does add some sodium to the water (not enough to worry about for most of us). And softened water shouldn't be used to water either indoor or outdoor plants.

Of all the moves you can make to increase your cleaning effectiveness, water softening equipment is one of the smartest. You'll want to weigh your own cleaning time and cost against how hard your water actually is, of course. If it's less than four grains per gallon, like our Hawaiian water, I'd forget it. If it's over ten grains per gallon, as in our Idaho home, I'd invest.

Any secrets for all of us who have to do our cleaning at night these days **?** ● *#26*

Welcome to the club. Ninety percent of all professional cleaning is done at night. Home cleaners, however, face the exact opposite situation of those pro janitors cleaning quietly in empty offices. At home, most everyone's there in the evening and in the way or up to something—cooking, eating, watching TV, doing homework, or elbow-deep in some overdue messy project. Which means we can either 1) move 'em all to one out of the way spot; 2) wait till they, at least the kids, are asleep; or 3) (the best choice) enlist them all into straightening up at least the new layer of litter they just created before they head off to bed and leave us with the rest.

Cleaning right under, over, around, and through them—if that's what you end up doing—may annoy them a little, especially when the vacuum snows up the TV. But at least they **see** you cleaning so they're less likely to grow up thinking that messes are dematerialized by invisible little elves.

We night cleaners are definitely at a disadvantage, since ambition doesn't peak in the P.M. for most of us and there's no real substitute for the nice, crisp, militant feel of an early start on a sunny morning. And you can't beat daylight for actually seeing what you're doing. We can't even fling open the windows and curtains when we start—unless we don't mind being exposed to all those dark shadows and passersby. Nor can we make much noise, unless we want to advertise our efforts or rouse Rover out back.

But don't think night cleaning is without its compensations:

• In the summer, it's cooler and just plain easier to face.

• Sunstreaks are no problem for us.

• There are fewer doorbell interruptions at night, though you still have to stay off the phone.

• Energy (to run washers, dryers, dishwashers, etc.) is cheaper during these "off peak" hours.

• After they do all go to bed, there's less tracking over wet floors and reusing of things before they're really ready. So wax gets a chance to dry, etc.

• And we can glory in the sensation that when we finish something it'll stay clean for at least six or eight whole hours!

• And right up there with the sheer sensual pleasure of crawling between clean sheets is putting out the light in a clean house . . . and waking up to a clean house!

But as for secrets of better night cleaning, the only one is LIGHT—get all you can, or daylight will reveal much that you missed by the light of the moon.

This isn't easy, since ceiling fixtures went out of fashion and most lamps and light fixtures are designed to diffuse or focus light, not let it flood the room. So get yourself a clamp light with a sturdy 150 watt bulb, and you'll have your own bright portable ceiling fixture. If you resort to the old strategy of moving a lamp close and taking off the shade, you'll trip over it or drip on it and be sorry.

Another aid for getting into those dingy corners is the headlight on your upright vacuum—unless the bulb burned out so long ago you forgot you had one.

To assist visibility, too, you can sometimes use a cleaner that makes it easier to see where you've been and where you're going. When pro window cleaners have to clean windows at night, they add a few drops of a sudsing detergent like Joy to the cleaning solution for this very reason.

We don't need to see well to straighten up, but if you do have to deep-clean an area at night, it helps if it's a place you've cleaned a lot previously. It's like driving a road you're familiar with after dark—at least you know where all the dips and curves and potholes and soft shoulders are.

Some things are unquestionably better candidates for night cleaning than others:

• In brightly lit rooms like the kitchen and bathroom, you can usually wield your sponge or mop at will. You can, unfortunately, even see well enough to clean out the refrigerator. Mood rooms like the living room are harder.

• Limited-area undertakings like polishing silver or reorganizing a drawer are no problem—as long as you can marshall the **will** to do them at midnight.

• Avoid things like wall or ceiling washing or waxing or painting or anything where thorough coverage is critical. It's too hard to see the skips or "holidays."

• A good job of grease removal is hard to do at night, too. And keep in mind that things take longer to dry at night when it's cooler and more humid.

• Windows, in case you wondered, are almost impossible at night. Rewipe as you will, streaks will always be revealed at sunrise, which is precisely why many professional cleaning contracts forbid night window cleaning.

• Dusting at night—unless the area in question has a lot of lamps—is a little like spreading lime by moonlight. You have to consciously cover every inch, rather than fly by eye as we usually do.

• Unless you're angry, dejunking is harder at night, without the help of the cold light of day.

• And bed making—sheet changing especially—may be trickier at night, though any nurses' or self-defense training you may have will help out here.

Should I sweep, dust mop, or vacuum my hard surface floors ? • #27

All three will get the job done—but the dust mop wins my vote hands down. It's faster and easier than any alternative—I dust mop not only my wood floors and the vinyl in my kitchen and hall, but the smooth, sealed concrete in my garage and shop.

Brooms stir up dust into the air and flip little bits of stuff around, and they never get the ultra-fine particles that will eventually grind and dull the glossy finish on your floors. They're also not very good at reaching under things. Brooms are best for getting up big or heavy stuff like mud or gravel or for a quick sweep of a small area like a laundry room or bathroom.

Vacuums are thorough but awkward and noisy, and they beat up the

63

bases and corners of everything. And the best kind to use on hard floors—a canister—can be a real project to get out and assemble. But a vacuum does suck dirt out of cracks and corners better than a broom or dust mop, and you don't have to shake it out or pick up a dirt pile when you're finished. I'd say if the vacuum is already out and you only need to do a small area, by all means use the vacuum. But for a floor of any size you can't beat a dust mop for speed and efficiency.

The reason many hard floor owners don't dust mop is because they've never owned a real dust mop, nor do they know how to prepare or take care of one. Most of the supermarket models just redistribute the dirt. Go to the nearest janitorial-supply store—the Yellow Pages will tell you exactly where—and buy yourself a professional-quality cotton dust mop with an eighteen-inch head and a swivel handle. Be sure to get a can or bottle of professional dust-mop treatment, too, so you can be sure your mop will pick up and hold the finest dust. You don't apply the mop treatment to the strands or edges of the mop, but to the thick, absorbent backing material. This provides a little reservoir of dust treatment that will wick down into the strands and make them attract dust like a magnet, without getting oily or sticky. After treating, hang the mop up for at least twelve hours before you use it, to give the wicking action a chance to happen, and **always** hang your dust mop up to store it.

Now to use it the way the pros do, push it ahead of you in one long, continuous S-stroke, swiveling from side to side as far as you can comfortably reach. Keep the mop head in constant contact with the floor, and always keep the same edge forward—if you lift or reverse the mop, you'll lose the little line of dust you're pushing and drop it on the already-cleaned area. Make one last swoop all around the edges of the room to finish the job. (See illustration)

Shake, comb, or vacuum the head out as soon as it gets fuzzed up (full of dust) and retreat it with dust-mop treatment whenever it seems to be losing its pickup power.

P.S. If you decide to use your vacuum on a hard surface floor, be sure to use the hard floor attachment, a simple suction tool with bristles. Never use a beater bar or power head on hard floors—the metal beaters can scratch and gouge vinyl, wood, or tile, and it won't do anything beneficial for the beater, either.

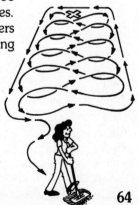

How do I clean a crystal chandelier ? ● #28

I ask myself this all over again every time I contract to clean a classy restaurant or new car dealership. Unfortunately, I already know the answer—*by hand*. Over the years, I've tried about every method, including the dip, spray, and drip-dry techniques, and it still gets down to polishing each individual crystal by hand if you want really first-class results.

The chandelier I lost my innocence to was the huge one that hangs in the famous Duchin Room at Sun Valley Idaho. Having no idea of how to bid the awesome fixture with its thousands of twinkling crystals, I made the restaurant owners a deal. Two of my managers and I and our wives agreed to clean the thing in exchange for a fancy dinner for all of us in the world-renowned dining room. We earned our meal—more like a week's room and board! Here's what I learned on that job and on others since:

Chandeliers collect a lot of cooking grease, dust, lint, fuzz, flyspecks, and cigarette smoke from the air. If you catch them before they get badly soiled, it is possible to "drip-clean" them to a degree. Make sure the electric power to the unit is off, and start by vacuum dusting to remove all the loose stuff. If the bulbs and sockets point up, put a sandwich bag over each one and secure it with a rubber band to prevent water from running down into the socket. Put a plastic dropcloth on the floor underneath to catch the runoff and cover it with newspapers or towels. Lighting dealers have ready-made chandelier cleaning solutions available such as Sparkle Plenty, or you can mix your own using one part isopropyl alcohol to three parts distilled water. This solution should be safe for the metal as well as glass or plastic of most fixtures. Spray a generous amount of the cleaner over the entire chandelier until it runs and drips from every pendant. Try to stay away from wires and bulbs and sockets, but make sure every pendant is thoroughly wet on every side. The crystals should drip dry without spots or streaks, although there may be a slight film on the surface. You can minimize this by getting up on a sturdy ladder and buffing the crystals with a soft cloth after the solution's been on there a while. After the crystals are clean and dry, finish up by removing the plastic bags and hand-wiping the saucers and any noncrystal parts of the fixture with a cloth dampened in the solution. Then let the whole chandelier dry overnight before turning on the power.

This method will do a decent job on a not-too-dirty chandelier. But for a heavily soiled fixture or one where you need a super-sparkle shine like they did in the Duchin Room, there's no substitute for hand polishing. You can spray and wipe the pendants in place or disassemble, depending on the size and configuration of the fixture. If you elect to polish in place, work your way from top to bottom, being careful not to put pressure on the wires that attach the pendants—some of these are pretty delicate. So don't pull on them—hold each pendant in place with one hand while you wipe or polish with the other.

To do a thorough job you can take the whole thing apart and individually polish each piece, but plan to spend some time on this. To avoid scratching or breaking the prisms, use one plastic tub for the washing solution and another one for a clear-water rinse. Carefully take down a dozen or so pendants (or one tier) and lay them in the bottom of the first tub—not in a pile or touching each other—and let them soak for as long as it seems to take to dissolve all the dirt. Then dip them into the rinse tub and finish by polishing with a clean, dry towel. Put the cleaned prisms back in place on the chandelier and continue in this fashion. If you take it all apart at once, you may have trouble remembering how it all goes back together!

Is there any way to really get rid of those tough odors and stains like urine, vomit and pet stains ? ● #29

There's no doubt that some of the toughest cleaning jobs we face are messes of "organic" origin—such as stains from pet or human potty accidents, urine, vomit, blood, skunk odor, spilled or spoiled food, or garbage. Materials like these often sink deep into the carpet, upholstery, concrete, and other surfaces—they have strong odors, and they provide excellent fuel for bacteria and fungus growth that creates a second source of odor and stain. It's almost impossible to get odors like these entirely out using ordinary cleaners, deodorizers, and detergents, and even steam cleaning or carpet shampooing won't do it.

For a long time professionals didn't have any 100 percent effective way to deal with them either. But then not long ago, out of the dairy and sewage treatment industries came a way to fight organic with organic—something unique among cleaning preparations—a **live** cleaner. Bacteria/enzyme digesters we call them.

When you mix up a batch of the digester it's actually a solution of live, friendly bacteria that feed on the source of the odor and stain. The bacteria keep on reproducing and keep on producing enzymes that digest the deposit until it's all gone from even the most deeply embedded areas, like carpet padding and backing. They're completely nontoxic and biodegradable, and they don't just mask or dilute the mess—they eliminate it.

You do have to follow the directions carefully, but all in all they're an incredible assist with the awfullest and most menacing messes. They can be used on any water-safe surface, and that includes carpet, drapes, upholstery, mattresses, foam rubber, clothing, and athletic wear (smelly sneakers!), tile grout, trash containers, garbage disposals, metal, plastic, vinyl, concrete, terrazzo, sealed wood, grass, and shrubbery. They can be used to fuel pet stool digesters and deodorize cages, dog runs, and kennels. They can banish fish slime and rotten bait odors and make it pleasanter to pull out the RV porta-potty. You can even buy bacteria/enzyme digesters specifically designed to snack their way through the coffee grounds, grease, soap scum, hair, and paper that often clog house drains and sewage lines.

So what's the catch? Well, like anything else alive bacteria/enzyme digesters do have a few peculiarities. You can't really use them when it's under fifty degrees or over one hundred degrees, and they work pretty slowly by spray-and-wipe standards—the process may take anywhere from six to twenty-four hours. And you have to keep the area wet—with the aid of a damp towel or piece of plastic—the whole time they're working. You have to use the solution within ten hours of mixing it up, or it won't be any good. The bacteria will have starved to death. And you can't use them with any soap or detergent or disinfectant or anyplace one of these things has been used recently without rinsing first—because this too will be lethal to your little bacteria helpers. Bacteria/enzyme digesters will usually remove all the odor, but sometimes a slight stain will remain, and a regular cleaner or spot remover will be needed to finish up the job.

Where do we find this wonderful stuff? Not in the supermarket or discount or department store, as you've probably noticed. Bacteria/enzyme digesters will be in all these places someday, but for now you'll probably have to go to a janitorial-supply store or pet shop or pet supply catalog to get one. They have names like Outright Pet Odor Eliminator, Enzyme Army, and Liquid Alive, and if you explain to the person in charge that it's a **bacteria/enzyme** (not just enzyme) product you're after, they'll be able to help assure that you leave with a smile on your face and the right bottle or container under your arm.

P.S. Be sure to remove all the loose material or liquid you can first, before applying the solution. Why use enzymes to remove anything a sponge or dustpan will?

Where is the best place to store cleaning supplies and equipment ? ○ #30

"Under the kitchen sink" isn't the answer—yet most of us have the entire supermarket aisle selection under there, nice and handy for breaking our back and bumping our head and for the little ones to get into. There's bottles, cans, tins, boxes, and jars stretching all the way back to where they poke into the insulation or have to be pulled out from beneath the plumbing. There's stuff resting on top of stuff, spilled stuff, and stuff knocked on its side and out of sight, mind, and action. And the whole assemblage is in an excellent position to be leaked on by aforesaid plumbing, rusting cans, disintegrating labels, and converting boxed cleaners into unidentifiable white lumps surrounded by soggy cardboard.

69

This is definitely not my favorite storage place for the cleaning goodies. If we just removed all the snoutless aerosols, anything that's rusted shut or ruined by water leaks, the accidental duplicates, the free samples we'll never get around to trying, bottles and jugs with about a tablespoonful still in them, and the stuff so old it's curdled, separated, or a collector's item, we'd be able to reduce the volume by half here. You should then be able to move about 60 percent of what's left—the necessary but seldom-used things—to a cleaning supply cache in the utility room or garage. Store your bulk cleaning supplies there, too, and put all those poisonous compounds with which our cleaning arsenal abounds up in a high, securely closed cupboard.

Central storage isn't necessarily what you're after. It makes much more sense to keep as much cleaning equipment as possible right where you use it. This means white nylon scrub sponge, all-purpose cleaner, angle broom, dustpan, and sponge mop in the kitchen, push broom and wet/dry vac in the garage, dustpan in the entryway, etc., and a little maid basket (see illustration) with the most-used cleaning supplies, including a spray bottle of disinfectant cleaner, in each bathroom. This really reduces the clutter under the sink and saves a lot of steps and trips, too. If you have a steep-staired house, you might even want one vacuum on each floor. Most cleaning supplies and equipment are inexpensive, and buying more than one of each costs out to a lot cheaper than all the time you waste struggling with inconvenient storage. And cleaning chemicals in little premeasured envelopes (see p. 117) make decentralized storage a cinch.

You need a roomy, easy-to-reach place, too, for large, frequently used tools like brooms, vacuums, and that safely designed step stool to stand on. Awkwardly stored or inaccessible vacuums are the biggest killer of the cleaning impulse going! You want to be able to roll that vacuum out easily, not wrestle it out from behind things, and if it's a canister you'll want some coat hooks, too, to hang the wand and hose. You have no space for this, you say? We never fail to find space for a coat closet—yet we probably use our cleaning supplies a lot more!

A first-class cleaning cupboard has a couple of good coats of enamel paint on the walls and no carpet on the floor, of course. And you wouldn't want it to be without a louvered door or other means of ventilation to speed the dryout of damp and soggy things.

Hanging things up is an especially good idea when it comes to cleaning supplies. Suspended wire baskets will do a dust-and-mildew-free job of organizing your sponge and cleaning cloth supply and the inevitable little odds and ends. If there's a place to hang up brooms, mops, etc., you're much less likely to leave them around or trip over them, plus you can find them when you need them. Most cleaning tools—brooms, mops, squeegees, and brushes, especially—keep their shape better, work better, and last longer if they're hung rather than jammed or crammed in. Hanging a dust mop also keeps the oily dust treatment you should be using on it from staining the walls. Of the many kinds of broom and tool hooks available, the Bassick hooks are about the best I've found.

Especially if you're short of space, streamline your equipment whenever you can. For example, the Doodlebug or Scrubbee Doo, a long-handled floor scrubber with interchangeable dust mop and waxer heads, is five tools in one. It's a pleasure to use, and it stores a lot more compactly than half a dozen different contraptions. I have a four-thousand-square-foot home and don't even have a floor machine here, only that little twenty-dollar tool.

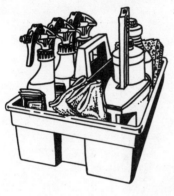

Is there any way to get that awful soap scum off the tub and shower walls ? ● #31

Ah yes, that sinister mixture of body oil, soap residue, and hard water scale that you might call the tooth plaque of the bathroom tile. After a subtle, inconspicuous start it just keeps building up, especially on the bottom two or three feet, and getting grayer and rougher and uglier all the time.

As with so many cleaning problems, the best offense is a good defense—in this case by preventing the dread stuff from forming in the first place.

If you have sliding glass shower doors, the first thing you'll want to do is consider ripping them out. When I finally built a new bathroom in my Sun Valley home, I installed nice smooth-sliding frosted shower doors, like we all aspired to. I soon discovered that keeping them looking first-class involved a lot of low-class labor. The tracks were always yucky, and soap scum covered the doors almost immediately and stuck to the glass like glue.

It was soon clear to me why even the best of hotels still use the humble shower curtain—it can be quickly and easily taken down and a fresh, clean one hung in its place. You can just throw the curtain in the wash and the tub and shower are easier to use, too.

If you have a fiberglass tub/shower enclosure, waxing it with automobile wax after cleaning will leave a slick, shiny surface that helps repel soap scum buildup and hard water scale. Ceramic tile walls can be wiped down with lemon oil for the same effect.

It will also help keep solids from accumulating if you hang a fourteen-inch window squeegee in the shower so bathers can quickly whisk the water off the walls as they step out. Some soaps also tend to leave less scum than others; one of the best for avoiding buildup in showers is Zest.

After all this prevention, you'll still have to face an accumulation of scum and scale from time to time. The first attack should be with a good soap scum remover. Most janitorial-supply houses sell a product specifically designed to remove the fats and oils that make up so much of this armorlike plating, and one of the best is Scum Clean from National Sanitary Supply. If you can't get your hands on one of these specialty products, any good degreaser (see p. 78) should work fairly well. The real secret is in letting the solution work before you start scrubbing. For heavy buildup, it can take fifteen minutes or more for the solution to penetrate and soften the scum, so wet it down and leave it to soak while you're doing something else. You may have to rewet it from time to time to keep it moist. Once it's softened up, scrubbing it off with a stiff brush or white nylon-backed scrub pad and rinsing takes no time at all.

In areas with hard water, you may also need to apply a phosphoric acid tub and tile cleaner, because the scum remover won't take off the hardwater scale. On the other hand, depending on the bath soap you use and the hardness of your water, the tub 'n' tile cleaner may take off both hard water and soap scum. It's always worth a shot to try the tile cleaner first by itself, especially if you don't have too bad a buildup. Often hard water deposits build up in little half-moon "shelves" of mineral on the walls, which then collect body oils and soap scum. Dissolving the shelves may bring the whole gooey mess sliding right down into the drain!

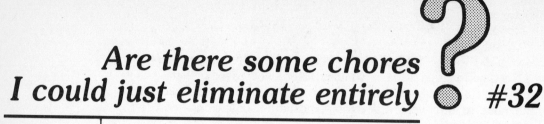

Are there some chores I could just eliminate entirely ? #32

Without a doubt! "Overkill"—totally unnecessary overcleaning—is almost as common as dirt. Times change, things change, you change, and your household has changed. The traffic patterns in your house aren't the same as they were ten years ago. If you've been caught up in long-established cleaning habits and schedules, stop and think about it a little. Many of us are still sweeping, dusting, and polishing things *that are never used and don't need it!* Mindlessly disciplined habits may have their place in the army, but in your own home, where you can do things your own way, you should only clean things that really need cleaning.

I'm not advocating ignoring dirt, junk, or filth, I'm just telling you, as a professional cleaner, that many things don't even need cleaning for months or weeks or years. And in our disposable society many things aren't even worth cleaning. Some housework that's burning up a lot of hours and human and kilowatt energy doesn't really need to be done often—or at all. There are more interesting ways to get exercise, if that's what you're after.

Let's have some examples here:

Overwashing. The average family uses two thousand towels in a year—that's a lot of laundry. Used towels aren't dirty; they're wet—they don't have to be tossed right in the hamper. Likewise, many people throw their work/yard clothes or children's play clothes in the wash after a single wearing.

Vacuuming. There must be something seductive about the hum and vibration of a vacuum, because many people vacuum almost twice as much as they need to. High-traffic areas might need daily or every-other-day vacuuming, but bedrooms only need a weekly going over— and some parts of a home need only be done once a month! Our workplaces and yards have changed drastically in twenty years; most of us only have to contend with a grass-covered yard today, not a mud-generating, dirt and gravel scattering barnyard. New and better door-mats (which you should install—see p. 18) keep most dirt and damage out. Today's carpets come with stain and soil blockers built right in. A lot of vacuuming done today is a total waste of time and electricity unless you count it as entertainment.

Windows. We all have a fetish about windows. Why? Windows are nondepreciating; no matter how dirty they get, they don't rot, wear out, stink, or deteriorate. Most glass, even when dirty, looks clean enough so you don't have to wash it every week or every month or because the neighbors do. When windows become visually offensive, clean them. If they don't bother you and the light can still penetrate and people can still find their way around inside, leave the windows unwashed and enjoy life a little.

Bathrooms. Bathrooms, with all their hard surfaces, are basically the cleanest, most sanitary rooms in the house. Bathrooms almost clean themselves, if you think about it. Whenever we use them it generally involves soap and water. That little bit of mineral (hard water) buildup on things isn't dirt. And who of us give tours of our shower stalls?

Floors. Here's one thing you can adjust out of your life for sure. Hard floors that have the right finish applied to them (professional grade of wax or sealer) will look good for a long time with only light mainte-nance. The floors in some of the commercial buildings we clean still have the same wax we put on them five years ago. Overwaxing, especially of corners and edges and other nontraffic areas, only creates unsightly wax buildup that has to be removed by the tiring and time-consuming process known as stripping.

The biggest secret of floor care is not to let dirt, gravel, sand, etc., ever get on the floor in the first place to grind off the shine. If you mat all the entrances to a home (see p. 18). You can go for years without scrubbing or stripping.

Shampooing. We've gone eight years in our ranch home without cleaning our carpet, and I have a carpet shampooer downstairs and professional truck-mount units available free at the snap of a finger! With good doormats and regular vacuuming and spot-cleaning, a normal home can go two to three years between shampooing, much upholstery even longer.

Polishing and shining metal that will only tarnish again, such as silver, brass, and copper—otherwise known as vanity cleaning.

Polishing furniture. Some people do it every time they dust—which only adds a quarter-inch of streaky gunk on the surface.

For that matter, **cleaning anything blackened**—from the barbecue grill to the aluminum pot you cook the artichokes in—that will shortly only be blackened again.

The twice-yearly washing of everything in the upper cupboards and china closet. Yes, that stuff does get dusty and grease-filmed, but why not just wait till you need something to serve company?

Washing walls. With today's much cleaner forms of heating and cooking, the walls in most homes don't need to be cleaned nearly as often as they used to.

Tidying up the fireplace every time you use it. How will anyone know that you've even had a fire? Just pull the screen shut.

Dusting endlessly. If your dust conditions are such that the knick-knack shelf needs a redo every other day, you might want to consider a glass-enclosed cabinet. Or even learning to live with a slight white film on everything above eye level. At least stop picking things up to dust under them! And see p. 55 for some dust control measures.

Drying dishes. Unless you're the washer and you just want company. Otherwise, let the dish drainer do what it was designed for.

Removing footprints from carpet and rump prints from plush or velvet furniture.

Playing bodyguard and handmaiden to special delicate objects and decorations and furnishings from white cotton rugs to delicate brocades to silk anything—unless they're the light of your life.

Making beds. If you haven't already, switch from six layers of top sheets and light blankets topped by a bulky bedspread to a single comforter that serves as both decoration and insulation and can be made up in a minute.

Ironing anything you don't have to.

Mending clothes. Unless they're into "quaint," who—including you—will ever be caught dead wearing the result?

What should I use to clean something really greasy *#33*

27ᵗʰ ANNUAL NATIONAL DEEP-FRIED ONION RING AND CRINKLE CUT COOK-OFF FINALS

Without the right kind of cleaner no amount of elbow grease is going to do it! The mild cleaners we **should** use as our all-purpose cleaners are "neutral"; they have a pH of 7 to 9—only slightly alkaline. This enables them to do most jobs fairly well without dulling waxes or damaging finishes. Grease deposits are an unusually acid kind of soil, however, so you need a more strongly alkaline cleaner (pH of 11–13)—or maybe even a solvent—to dissolve and remove them. A good degreaser has a high enough pH to "emulsify" (dissolve) fat, oil, and grease—breaking it down from a solid slick into tiny floating globs that can be whisked away in the washwater. Oven cleaner is a good example of this principle. Most of that stuff caked on ovens is solid fat, and Easy-Off and the like are caustically alkaline (pH 14) so they eat it off quick. But you don't want to use oven cleaner outside the oven.

When we think of grease cutting, ammonia also comes to mind, and it is alkaline, so it removes grease pretty well. But ammonia isn't the safest or best-smelling thing to be sloshing around with, and it can damage some of the household surfaces, as well as human surfaces, it comes in contact with.

Believe it or not, plain old dish detergent is fully up to the job of dealing with many grease problems in the home. After all, it was designed to cut cooking grease from pots and pans. The secret is **time**— spray the solution on, let it soak for ten seconds or so, and presto, the grease dissolves, and you can wipe it away.

If you have cooked on grease or a really heavy accumulation, an industrial strength degreaser will cook its goose fast. My favorite is the butyl cleaner you can find at a janitorial-supply store. Butyl cleaners are powerful degreasers if you don't mind a few fumes. They'll shear right through the skin oils, hand lotion, food smears, etc., that cling to and around kitchen cupboard hardware and other heavily handled places around the home.

You might like one of the newer heavy-duty degreasers, too—a product called Soilmaster. It comes in concentrated form and has a citrus oil base that really rips the grease. Since it's a non butyl cleaner, it has no petroleum solvents or disagreeable odors and it's very safe to use.

When you're degreasing, don't fight with greasy vents or grilles in place; just remove them. Wipe off what you can with paper towels, then set the unit in the sink to soak in a hot degreasing solution; the chemical will do the work for you. Then scrub lightly with a nylon scrub pad or a brush and then rinse with hot water.

Grease in kitchens is inescapable, so keep absorbent surfaces like wallpaper, carpeting, and drapes as far from the grease drift zone as possible. And downdraft stove venting units are well worth the money. Stove-level grease suction is far superior to a hood or ceiling unit, according to my grease gauge.

P.S. If it's a grease stain in carpeting or car upholstery that you're grappling with, use a solvent like dry cleaning fluid.

How can I remove a heavy crust of "hard water" deposits from a faucet, shower door, or other surface ? ● #34

Much of our tap water is "hard" which means it contains dissolved minerals (rocks!). The most frequent offender is calcium carbonate, which the groundwater leaches out of limestone. When the H_2O evaporates from a drop, splash, or drip, where does the mineral go? You guessed it—it doesn't go; it remains, a faint, milky film at first, but it keeps on accumulating with each additional splash, drip, flush, or spray and gradually builds up into a deposit, exactly like the tartar on our teeth. One or two days' worth of hard water residue can be wiped off with almost anything, but after a week (or a month or a year) or two you're chipping away at a little block of mineral, like a hunk of cement. Just as a toothbrush won't remove tartar, neither will a brush or everyday cleaning solution remove hard water deposits.

I don't want to give you any more bad news, but when it comes to bathroom fixtures you have a dash of body oil and a pinch of soap scum blended into that deposit, too—actually three meanies clinging to the chrome. Chemical attack—dissolving—is the answer, and since this partic-

79

ular soil is alkaline, it takes an acid cleaner to cut it. This is why most tub and tile cleaners and lime removers contain phosphoric acid, which is o.k. to use on chrome faucets and most other bathroom surfaces as long as you rinse it off afterward. The lime scale removers available in supermarkets are about a 4 percent phosphoric solution, while the professional-strength ones available at janitorial-supply stores will be 8 or 9 percent or even stronger. I wouldn't recommend anything above a 10 percent phosphoric for home use, but an 8 or 9 percent solution is relatively safe to use and will work much faster and better than a weaker product. The best such cleaner I've found is Showers-n-Stuff, a blend of phosphoric and other buffered acids. It can be used full-strength for heavy-duty descaling, then diluted for daily maintenance of all bathroom fixtures. Regular cleaning with a 1:10 solution of Showers-n-Stuff and water will keep lime scale at bay and eliminate desperation descaling in the future.

When you do use Showers-n-Stuff or a similar product full-strength for the initial buildup removal, let it sit on there and work awhile, then bring on a white nylon-backed scrub sponge to assist the chemical action. Wear rubber gloves to protect your hands, and be sure to rinse well when you're done to avoid damaging tile grout, chrome, and other surfaces.

For the hard-water deposit known as toilet bowl ring you may need a stronger acid cleaner. Bowl cleaners made from phosphoric acid are again the safest kind to use, even though stronger acids may work faster. If you use a bowl cleaner containing hydrochloric or sulfuric acid, be extremely careful—they can damage carpet, metal, enamel, clothing, and furnishings and skin very rapidly. And any toilet bowl cleaner should be used **only** in the toilet bowl—it's too dangerous to use anywhere else. When you're using an acid bowl cleaner, bear in mind that pouring it into a bowl full of water dilutes the chemical down far too much for it to have any impact. So push the water down into the throat of the fixture by pumping your bowl swab up and down energetically there first to force the water out of the trap and lower the water level in the bowl. Then you can wring out your swab and use it to apply **full-strength** bowl cleaner to the ring and up under the rim. Let the acid work for several minutes, reapply if necessary, then finish swabbing the rest of the bowl and flush. If the ring is too well established and stubborn to respond to bowl cleaner, a brisk rubdown with a pumice bar will remove it without hurting the toilet—just be sure to keep the area wet while you're scrubbing on it. Regular use of an acid bowl cleaner thereafter will keep a ring from re-forming.

P.S. And use of an automatic bowl cleaner like 2000 Flushes will do a lot to extend the time between scrubbings.

How do I clean a baseball cap ● *#35*

... assuming I can ever get my husband/kid/boyfriend parted from his long enough to clean it

You mean you'd like to know how to clean that dirty "gimmie" cap, those promo giveaways? *Answer:* toss it in the washing machine!

Next question: how do you straighten a clean, deformed gimmie cap? *Answer:* Where is that booth or store or company? Go back there and act interested and get a new one!

Seriously, though, these are often free or cheap, so the most logical approach is to simply wear it till it uglies out and then toss it. But if you have a real favorite or one of the more deluxe editions that actually did cost you a pretty penny, here's how to go about cleaning it:

If it's a well-made, fairly expensive cap made of wool or corduroy, I'd pack it off to the dry cleaners. Or you can hand-wash it gently in cool water and Woolite, then rinse it and set it on a towel to air dry. Carefully remold it to its proper shape before it starts the drying process, using a rolled up towel or a small pot, bowl, or coffee can to hold it up or round it out, if necessary.

If it's a polyester, nylon, polycotton, or poplin cap with lettering or appliques or embroidery on it (many of these have nylon or polyfoam incorporated into them somewhere, too), how you approach cleaning it has a lot to do with how dear it is to your heart.

• The most conservative approach—for hats with wings, antlers, wolf noses, or miniature beer cans attached, the one from the place you'll never manage to visit again, or the one personally signed by your favorite country singer: vacuum it first if it's very dusty and then just wipe it down with a cloth dampened in hand dishwashing detergent solution or other mild cleaner. Keep off that autograph, though.

• If it's unquestionably gonna take more than that, the following method is enthusiastically endorsed by not a few hat manufacturers and cap fanciers alike: put it on the top rack of the dishwasher—no dishes allowed—add a little bit of dishwasher detergent and run through the normal cycle, BUT snatch it back out before the dry cycle begins and all the heat sets in. Then hand block as described above and let it air dry.

• If you're willing to be a little more daring you can also try washing caps in the regular clothes washer, with Woolite and cold water, on the **gentle** cycle. Spray the headband and bill (which are often the oiliest and blackest parts) with laundry pretreat first and put the cap in a mesh laundry bag. Another way to protect the lettering and the bill is to turn the cap inside out and tuck the bill up under the band in the back.

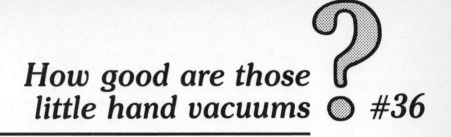

How good are those little hand vacuums ? ● #36

I own four of them now! But my first impression of them was another matter. They had such a puny capacity compared to the enormous super suction models I'd grown up with in commercial cleaning, surely those tiny inexpensive things could be of little use.

Then one was left as a gift at our guest house in Hawaii. I sneered at it for several days until some sandpapering on a sticking door left a few stripes of sawdust. It was right at my elbow, so I risked it—a minute later my mess was gone. At lunchtime that same day, a visitor scuffing his feet under our table left a little pile of coral sand. Again the little vac was handy, and the floor was restored. After breakfast the next morning the usual crumbs surrounding the toaster were quickly disposed of with the little handheld sitting there on the counter.

My conversion only proceeded faster as I realized this was the perfect picker-upper for those dropped ashes and elusive drawer crumbs, the dead bugs on the windowsill, that final low-profile floor pile after the dustpan has done its best. Cordless vacs are available, too, with power brush attachments (miniature beater bars) that give them the extra muscle they need to take on upholstered furniture, carpeted stairs, car interiors, and the pet's favorite napping place. They have their own crevice tools and upholstery brushes, too, for anywhere that can't be reached by even a cordless's slender snout. These mighty midgets have even caused me to do something we should all do more, and that's **clean as we go**—get the mess now instead of when it's big and demoralizing and spread all over. A cordless is so light and maneuverable and quiet you don't "dread dragging it out." And the second you come across it, you can get snack food fallout, kicked-out kitty litter, spilled flour or cereal, dried mud, or scattered potting soil right out of your life. In short, speed and handiness more than compensate for smallness. The small size of the bag is a plus in the end because you can empty it right inside the house without causing a three-layers-of-newspaper vacuum emptying event.

The cordless feature is the biggest secret of their success, of course. On most small vacuuming jobs we spend more time plugging in and unplugging and replugging (after the plug pulls out) and controlling the cord than vacuuming. A handheld vac eliminates this entirely; it mounts on the wall anywhere there's an electrical source, inside or outside a closet. Black & Decker's Dustbuster started it all, but now a number of other manufacturers have come out with their own cordless handheld wonders until it's almost hard to choose. Home and professional vacuumers are so happy to have cut the cord, they've also given a warm welcome to the big brother of the cordless handheld—the cordless upright such as the Eureka New Freedom. These won't do the deep, thorough job that does need to be done twice a month or so on carpet to prevent damage and deterioration, but they're terrific for daily traffic area maintenance or spot vacuuming. They're light and easy to handle and make a great second vacuum and touchup tool. What else is new in cordless vacs? I got my first double duty handheld wet/dry vacuum last week—I never thought I'd see the day I could vacuum up a dropped egg in less time than it takes to crack it!

Other people's dirt . . . is it as bad as we all imagine ❓ ⚫ *#37*

Most of us learned early how dirty the other person's germs are. "Don't you dare touch that gum stuck under the desk; one of those wretched Whomevers might have chewed it." Sharing your girl friend's all-day sucker never seemed too bad (or even your brother's or sister's), but strangers' stuff was definitely taboo! Our scout patrol had one toothbrush at camp until the scoutmaster explained that Tenderfoot and Eagle Scout germs are unmixable. By the time we were old enough to rent a room, dorm, or house, our germ paranoia was well developed.

So now as adults we all have something of a phobia about OPG—other people's germs.

In thirty-two years of commercial cleaning I've never come across a case of anyone being done in by other people's germs—their junk, swimming pool, stairway, or backyard swing maybe, but never their germs. Still, we all know this particular emotion isn't easily put to rest.

Here's what we pros do and what you can do to dispel all your doubts.

Dejunk. Before you buy or move in, have the present owner or the Realtor or lawyer put in the contract that they will get rid of all junk before they move out. This doesn't guarantee that they'll do it, because in the final hours of moving and packing the will or strength often fails. But it'll at least cut down on the amount of garbage left behind to house bugs and rodents or cause **you** the nuisance and expense of having it hauled away. Otherwise, in attics and garages and sheds and yard, you're all too likely to face piles of rotting wood and rusty metal, junk cars, tread bare tires, old refrigerators, broken lamps, cracked hoses, bags, cans and bottles of unidentified and potentially poisonous stuff—etc., etc., etc.

Disinfect: Even if the house is clean (or new), a quick disinfecting job is a good all-round conscience calmer. You know you're going to end up washing a good part of the place anyway (is one person's cleaning job ever good enough for another?). So go get a gallon of "quat" (see p. 123) disinfectant concentrate at the janitorial-supply store. It'll cost less than ten bucks, and you can make one hundred gallons of solution with it—plenty more than you'll need. Dilute it according to the directions on the label and with a spray bottle or mop and bucket quickly spray it on the bathroom fixtures, around the base of the toilet, and in all the corners, under the sinks. Don't forget the doorknobs and door frames, the washer and dryer, and the kitchen floor—any place that's had heavy human or animal contact **except** the kitchen cupboards and counters and appliances inside and out, which you'll want to clean with just a strong all-purpose cleaner and appropriate amount of elbow grease. Do let the disinfectant sit on all surfaces for five or ten minutes; in fact, it's not a bad idea to let it dry right on the surface in the worst places, anywhere moisture won't damage. This stuff destroys bacteria right in its breeding grounds and odors, too! I always spray the basement, too, to control mildew. If your fears are really ferocious, you can even wash the walls and utility room with the solution.

If the former occupants really dug deep frying, you might also want to use a degreaser (see p. 78) or hard-surface deodorizer such as Nilodor surface deodorizer. (You can add the deodorizer right to your disinfecting solution.) If you're left with a lingering tobacco odor, see p. 169. As for those gray areas like carpet and upholstered furniture, which most of us find it hard to be 100 percent comfortable with, rip it up and replace it if it's old and gross anyway. And have the rest shampooed, especially if they had pets.

When you move out, they won't believe you left it clean either, so leave the rest of that gallon of disinfectant behind so they can do their own thing.

How about some professional pointers on using a spray bottle ? ● #38

We're talking about the type of bottle you buy empty and fill with diluted concentrate yourself, of course. This way all you pay for is the bottle and the chemical. When you buy the ready-to-use variety, you're paying a premium for plain old water!

Applying cleaning solution with a spray bottle is a lot faster and easier than doing it with a cloth, and it all but eliminates dipping your hands into harsh chemicals. A sprayer also reaches all those little crannies and crevices better.

We professionals know how to work spray bottles to the max, so here's the inside scoop on spray bottle cleaning.

First, start with a healthy spray bottle—too many of them have **emphysema** (they wheeze and wheeze and little comes out), **collapsed lungs** (the side is caved in), **congestion** (the nozzle is plugged), or other respiratory ailments like nozzle drip. Go down to a janitorial-supply store and pick up five or six professional spray bottles with Continental or equivalent industrial quality trigger sprayers. They'll last ten times longer than those little squirts you get from the grocery or discount store. (Just never let your kid know how far and straight these babies shoot!) I like a quart size bottle because it lasts longer and doesn't fall over, but for smaller hands the twenty-two-ounce size is good.

Get the see-through kind, so you can easily see what's in them, and learn to color-code your cleaning chemicals. It's much less confusing—and safer—if the glass cleaner is always blue, disinfectant cleaner pink, all-purpose cleaner green, etc.

To avoid an unruly head of foam on your freshly filled bottle, fill the bottle with water **before** you add the cleaner concentrate—don't pour the water into the cleaner. Take advantage of those clever little lines on the side—graduations—to assure yourself an accurate mix. And the minute the bottle is filled, get a permanent magic marker and **write the name of the contents on the bottle.** If you don't, you'll be sorry. Lots of us have two or three spray bottles under the sink with some unidentified liquid in them. We're afraid to use them, but won't throw them out because "they might still be good." The hazard of unmarked bottles was well demonstrated by my daughter, who sprayed an unmarked cleaning solution on the rug to clean up a spot—*it was bleach!*

Don't ignore the fact that a spray bottle nozzle can be adjusted, usually by turning the tip, to alter the type of spray that comes out. It can produce a fine mist or a twenty-foot-long straight stream (excellent for water fights or waking dozing nonhousecleaners.) The coarser settings put more solution on the surface faster, and the fine spray is great for covering large areas, dampening clothes, and misting houseplants. Remember, however, that if you set your sprayer for a fine mist in a shower or other closed-in area, you'll be breathing atomized cleaning solution, a situation that's especially unhealthy when you're dealing with disinfectant or acidic cleaners. Out in the living room doing spot cleaning, the semimist setting is what you want to spritz over an eight-inch handprint and put just the right amount of moisture on so it won't run down the wall.

When you're spraying, don't overdo the point-blank approach. Blasting the target from two inches away means a lot of flooding and wasted solution, not to mention ricochets! You also want to watch overspray, like hitting the drapes, the carpet, the magazine rack, and the cat when all you were aiming at was a smudge on the coffee table. Take a second to be sure the nozzle is adjusted accordingly. Another way to avoid overspray, as well as to keep liquid out of electrical outlets and the like, is to spray the solution onto your cleaning cloth instead of directly onto the surface, when necessary.

Once the bottle gets below quarter-full, quit trying to fool it by holding it at odd angles and assuming grotesque positions to get the rest of the solution up the tube. I puzzled on how to solve this for the first ten years of my cleaning career and finally did—by simply refilling the bottle as soon as it gets down to a quarter-full.

When you're storing spray bottles, be sure to tighten down the spray nozzles to shut them off so the kids can't guzzle the contents.

If the sprayer won't work, unscrew the nozzle and poke the hole out with a needle—sometimes they do get plugged up. Or even more likely the ball valve—the thing you always hear rattling around in there—may be stuck so the pump isn't priming. The simple solution to this is to hit the trigger assembly against your hand a few times, then pump it vigorously while squeezing the bottle to prime it.

If and when the trigger sprayer pump is in need of a triple bypass—all flow has stopped—chuck it, but not the bottle. New trigger sprayers are sold separately—they're one of my housecleaning store's most popular sellers—for less than a dollar.

How do you clean off those labels manufacturers stick on everything without harming the finish or taking forever **?**

We all know the Murphy's law of labels and stickers:

• Labels containing essential directions self-destruct within two weeks—the ink smudges, the whole label falls off, or goop runs down the side of the bottle and obscures everything.

• Ditto for those few labels we wish would last indefinitely because of the exclusive source or location they reveal.

• Labels on mirrors, crystal goblets, and gifts, that we'd like to remove immediately, are always put on with some miracle glue they lost the antidote to.

• The price sticker always covers up something important that pulls

90

off right along with it. Or it'll be right in the middle of the flashlight lens, the face of your favorite singer, or the best burl on the myrtlewood bowl.

In more than thirty years of new-construction cleanup, I've removed labels and stickers from every imaginable surface from skyscraper windows to gold-plated bathroom faucets. Some labels are just plain hard to get rid of without doing damage to the underlying object. Trying to undo all this retail recklessness can get pretty frustrating, but there are a few things that can make the job easier:

• First see if you can get out of it easy. Lay a piece of regular, not "magic," cellophane tape over it and pull it up and off fast. Many a price sticker will come right along with it.

• Don't scrape! Resist the tendency to attack stickers with razor blades, putty knives, and screwdrivers—they can gouge, scratch, and gash. The only surfaces I'd scrape with steel tools are glass and porcelain and then only when the glass or porcelain is good and wet.

• Instead, start by soaking. Many labels are applied with water-soluble adhesives, which will release after soaking in warm, not hot, water for a few minutes. If the object itself can't be set in water, you can lay a wet washcloth or paper towel on the surface for a while.

• If water doesn't do it, try wetting the label with a solvent. My favorite is De-Solv-it, an orange-oil product. It's safe for most surfaces and it quickly dissolves and removes most label and tape adhesives, chewing gum, and other sticky situations. Baby oil (mineral oil) and WD-40 work, too, but take longer to soften the glue. Volatile solvents like nail polish remover acetone, dry cleaning fluid, or lacquer thinner will often work very well indeed on things like glass, porcelain, chrome, and aluminum, but will damage paint, plastics, and some metals, such as brass and bronze. Full-strength pine cleaner or laundry pretreat sprays are milder sorts of solvents that might do it. It often helps to peel as much of the label off as possible before applying the solvent. If the surface could stand it and it seems necessary, you could also lay a solvent-soaked rag over the spot, cover it with Saran Wrap, and leave it for a few hours.

• After the water or solvent has softened the adhesive, gently scrape the label off with your fingernail, a white nylon scrub sponge, or a soft nylon scraper. Use more of the appropriate solvent as necessary to remove any last traces of adhesive.

• Go especially easy when you're down to nothing but a glue scab on there—otherwise level-headed label removers have been known to lose their self-control this close to the goal and start to scrape too hard or splash the wrong stuff on there.

• Labels and stickers on wood, leather, and paper, printed or porous surfaces, and clear plastic call for extra caution, because you can't use solvents, or even water, in many cases.

• Large plastic decals and bumper stickers that resist soaking can be heated with the hot air from a blow dryer—this will usually soften the adhesive enough so they can be peeled off. Be careful not to get the underlying surface too hot, though, especially if it's paint or plastic, or you might just remove it, too.

• Those little adhesive foam pads used to mount "stick-up" room deodorizers, photos, and posters present a special challenge. If you're not careful, you end up removing little chunks of paint and plaster right along with them. The safest way to go about removing one of these is to slip a butter knife behind the object in question and slice through the foam as you pull the poster or whatever from the wall. This leaves half of the foam stuck to the object and half still on the wall. The remaining adhesive on the wall can usually be rolled up into balls with your thumb, like rubber cement, and plucked off. If not, De-Solv-it should soften the remaining glue. Don't use oily solvents on flat latex paint, though, or you'll leave a stain.

With a little caution and common sense, most labels and stickers can be removed without scathing the stickee. But if that "Celebrate the Bicentennial" bumper sticker has a lifetime guarantee, maybe a new chrome job isn't out of the question.

How can I clean the cactus and my other houseplants without harming them **?** ● #40

We can be thankful that cactus seem to shed dust, but that's more than we can say for all those other green-leafed lovelies that face up for a handout from the sun and the rain. They collect their share of dust and other household fallout and get to looking pretty shabby before you know it.

Dust and dirt on the leaves don't just dull the dieffenbachia; they block out the light and clog the thousands of tiny pores plants use to "breathe"—release water and oxygen to the air and take in the carbon dioxide they need to perform that famous old process of photosynthesis. No wonder a grimy houseplant grows slowly—it's starving as well as suffocating. So cleaning your plants is a good idea, but do remember

93

that you're cleaning them, not decorating them. Trying to make a live plant's leaves shine like a freshly waxed floor isn't going to do it any good, either. Stay away from commercial leaf shine products—or you'll just be exchanging one leaf-pore clogger for another. The same is true of the home brew leaf shine recipes you hear about, from skim milk to salad oil to glycerin. Whatever you smear on there and let dry is only going to gum up the works.

The safest and best thing to use on those leaves is plain old water. But if you just sit the plants in the shower, you can get too much water on them, and the force of some showers can easily blast potting soil all over and snap off a section or two of your prize peperomia.

So instead, do it like the pros do—fill a sturdy professional spray bottle with clear water, set the nozzle on a nice gentle spray setting, hold the bottle about two feet away, and shoot the plant all over. You can set your plants in the tub, outside, or on a piece of plastic to do this. Keep on spraying until the water drips and runs off all the leaves to be sure and flush away any accumulation—if you just get them barely wet they'll look good until they dry and no longer. Don't fail to spray the undersides of the leaves, too—there are more pores there than anywhere. This is also a great way to wash away uninvited insects and insect eggs, especially after your plants have been living it up outside for the summer.

You can hand wash large-leafed plants, if you insist—with a soft cloth dampened in a mild solution of dish detergent and water. Go easy when you do this, to keep down unintentional leaf amputations, and don't forget the bottoms of the leaves here, either. Use a fresh cloth on each plant (or a disposable tissue instead) if you want to be extra-sure not to spread plant diseases.

In between times, keep the worst of the dust and dirt off with an untreated (electrostatic) dust cloth (see p. 56), a soft-bristled brush, or a lambswool duster for floor to ceiling ficus and the like. This is one dusting chore where a feather duster might even make sense. It's fast and easy and the leaves look lusciously natural afterward.

Is rinsing really necessary **?** *#41*

One of my first professional jobs was cleaning supermarkets. Cleaning in this case included sweeping, mopping, scrubbing, and waxing an endless floor area, but, boy, could I make those grimy grocery floors shine! They mirrored the Cheerios by the time we left at 5:00 A.M. But then people actually walked on those gorgeous floors, pushed carts across them, and spilled things on them, and by evening my dazzling floors were destroyed. At least half of my beautiful wax would be walked off, and the floors would be dull and drab-looking again. I spent a fortune on wax to recoat them every night. And so went the battle—I cleaned and the customers ruined, over and over and over. I got so I hated people with legs!

Then one night I learned something that made the same effort on the same floor last for weeks instead of one night. It was a magic word called "rinse." For years when doing floors, like most of you still do, I'd scrub

95

hard and then give it a quick lick with rinse water or just let the floor dry after I mopped up the muck. It looked and felt clean but wasn't really rinsed, so a layer of alkaline residue from the soap or stripper was still there. Then when I applied wax to the floor (right over the residue) the wax would streak, yellow, powder, and slough off with just the tiniest bit of foot traffic. That detergent residue was keeping the wax from bonding tightly to the floor. Once I learned to rinse, the wax would stick like glue and last ten times longer.

I suffered with my floors for not rinsing, and so will you. Don't rinse the dishes and you risk a case of the runs; fail to rinse your clothes and you'll be rashy; forget about rinsing those vegetables and fruits and you may develop pesticide poisoning.

Why are we so often reluctant to rinse? Somewhere in our mental cleaning computer we build up a real allegiance to the cleaning solution. We figure it has all the power to do the job and once we've put it on there, anything else is just extra. But whether you're washing your hair or your clothes or even washing the old dog, when the cleaning is over, the job isn't! To prevent a cloudy, streaked finish—if not actual damage—there's always some residue that needs to be flushed away. This is especially true if the surface is badly soiled or you're using a strongly acid or alkaline cleaner or something "straight from the bottle" full strength. The mildest abrasive cleaner, unrinsed, will leave sharp, sandpapery little bits behind. Carpet and upholstery shampoo, unrinsed, leaves a sticky film that'll attract dirt five times faster than before it was applied. Even the most ordinary cleaning solution, unrinsed, evaporates down to a deposit that just sits on there and gets thicker and thicker every time you reclean and don't rinse. Before you know it, you've got a chemical sludge strong enough to etch and corrode.

The key to rinsing is clean water, of course, and often a rinsing chemical added to the water helps, too, like the rinsing agent you add to your dishwasher for those spotless glasses or the neutralizing rinse I learned to use on the supermarket floors. A vinegar solution— half a cup of white vinegar to a gallon of water—does a good job of removing most soap residues. Impatient as we always get with rinsing, don't forget that once may not be enough. And if you've got a really dirty job ahead of you, rinsing **before** you clean is a fine idea to flush away the loose litter and filth before you put sponge to floor or fender.

Rinsing is a nice habit to get into. It means you'll rinse out your paintbrushes when you're finished with them, so you won't have to beat them on the sidewalk to limber them up before you use them next time. You'll rinse our your weed sprayer when you're done with it, so the chemical won't crystallize and plug the nozzle. And rinsing is even a bargain. Plain water costs so little, and it can improve your cleaning efficiency infinitely.

I have a young family—what carpet holds up best against wear, spots, spills, and pets ? #42

First of all, it's nylon, no doubt about it. The latest generation of nylon carpet fibers can take twenty wild kids, four careless cats, and a hurricane or flood or two in stride. My hat's off to the carpet industry; they've managed to take the tough plastic called nylon and limber it up to the point that it's soft, plush, and luxurious. It's also long-wearing, mildew and crush resistant, mothproof, colorfast, and nonallergenic. The newer nylon fibers such as Stainblocker and Stainmaster even have the dye locked in with a heat process, so stains have a very hard time taking hold. Nylon is the most durable, stain-resistant, and pleasing of the easy-care man-made carpet fibers. I've cleaned carpets professionally for thirty years, and it's getting to be hard to tell a good nylon pile carpet from a rich wool one. Just stick to the better brands and bear in mind that in carpet and carpet padding you do get what you pay for. Take your carpet dealer's advice seriously—they're competent.

One critical issue to concentrate on is color. The more use and wear a carpet gets, the more you need to consider the principle of camouflage. That means get a color and pattern that disguises and conceals. And may I suggest a blend of colors, like gravy brown, Velveeta orange, butter yellow, lettuce green, etc. You could spill a whole taco salad in the living room and not notice it for a while. Reddish-brown tweeds are among the best hiders going. More family messes blend into that color than any I know of. Medium shades hide soiling best—extremely light or extremely dark colors will highlight every smudge and lint speck. Sculpturing or texturing helps, too. Solid colors and plush cut pile show dirt and abuse sooner and every footprint and vacuum track. And no, it isn't silly to consider a color that matches your pet, if he's a shameless shedder, or your sandy loam, if tracking in is the issue.

If in doubt, ask the dealer for the name of someone who has bought this type and color of carpet and call and ask him how he likes living with and cleaning it. Some of the most attractive carpets in the showroom sample stack don't hold their own on the living room floor.

For high-traffic areas like hallways, stairs, and family rooms, a dense, level loop pile carpeting wears best and cleans easiest. Nowadays many carpets come in a commercial level loop (the low, long-wearing pile made for stores and businesses) and in the same colors as the residential line—mix the two in your home and get the best of all worlds! If you want a velvet or plush pastel, put it in the master bedroom, where it'll at least have a chance.

P.S. If you do get one of the new stain-resistant fibers, follow the manufacturer's cleaning instructions carefully or have the job done by a pro who really knows what he's doing. Certain cleaning procedures—using too hot a water or high pH cleaners—can injure those expensive stain-repelling properties and void the warranty.

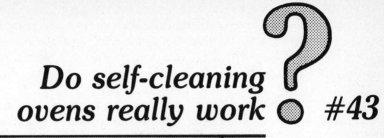

Do self-cleaning ovens really work ? #43

Yes, they do. In fact, they're cheaper as well as a lot easier to use than that messy and dangerous old-fashioned oven cleaner. But people often have problems with them because they don't use them properly. Frustrated homemakers ask me constantly, "How do I clean my self-cleaning oven?" Most of them are battling with baked-on food around the gasket or on the edges of the door. They know they shouldn't use caustic oven cleaners on self-cleaning ovens, but don't know how to get the gunk off.

Here's what happens: Self-cleaning ovens work by heating the oven interior so hot (eight hundred to one thousand degrees Fahrenheit) that any food residue in there is cremated or turns to ash, which merely has to be wiped away with a damp cloth or paper towel. Since the door gasket is a heat barrier, the self-cleaning feature only works from the gasket in—it won't take off food spilled on the door or on the oven frame outside the gasket.

The area just outside the gasket does get very hot, six hundred degrees or so, not hot enough to burn off any deposits, but much hotter than normal baking temperatures—enough to bake the food on so hard and tight that dynamite won't dent it. Then you're stuck with a super hard glaze of carbonized cherry cobbler on there, and you can't use oven cleaner to get it off. Why? Because the traces that'll be left behind no matter how hard you try to get it all off will damage the porcelain the next time you turn on the self-cleaning cycle.

So what do you do? Every instruction manual I've ever seen for a self-cleaning oven cautions you to clean off any food spilled outside the gasket before you use the self-clean cycle. This can be done with any heavy-duty cleaner or degreaser, which should be up to removing the incrustation if you do it before applying the high heat of the cleaning cycle. If you follow this procedure faithfully from the time your oven is new, you shouldn't have a serious problem. If you didn't read the little booklet and have a buildup barbecued on there now you're in trouble. Just about anything that will take it off easily will also damage the porcelain or the gasket (often made of fiberglass, so be sure to read the manual carefully now to see what you *can* safely use on it). You aren't going to get out of this without applying some elbow grease, but at least you know how to avoid the problem in the future.

Another problem sometimes reported by self-cleaning oven owners is failure of the oven to come completely clean. This is usually a simple matter of setting it for a longer cleaning cycle, although some of the less expensive self-cleaning ovens may never get quite hot enough to really do the job.

A couple of other cautions: If the oven racks are chrome or aluminum or anything other than porcelain-coated steel, and you want them to stay shiny and new-looking, don't leave them in during the self-cleaning cycle. The high heat will turn them blackish blue. If you don't want to clean the racks by hand and don't mind the tarnished look, leave them in—it doesn''t hurt anything but the appearance.

Also be careful about putting aluminum foil in the bottom of any oven, as it can burn out the heating element prematurely. Crinkles in the foil focus reflected heat back onto the heating element, creating hot spots. And don't cover oven racks completely with foil—it seals the oven into separate compartments, with the thermostat in one of them blissfully ignorant of the abnormally high temperatures that have built up in the other. One woman I know blew her oven door clear off this way!

How often should I empty the vacuum bag ❓ #44

I remember once, before I knew better, emptying the bag on our upright vacuum on the Fourth of July, and there was Christmas tinsel and New Year's caramel corn snuggled down in there, along with the watermelon seeds and float fragments. That's too long to wait, folks. The "empty-it-every-time-you-vacuum" club may be a little extreme, too, but twice a month isn't unreasonable. Tests show that by the time the bag is **one-quarter** full, vacuum suction is down 30 percent, so I'd always keep it dumped before it gets beyond the halfway point.

Capacity isn't the only dumping criterion, especially for those of us (most of us) in flea country. Regular vacuuming is a great means of flea control because you remove the new crops of flea eggs laid in the carpet before they can hatch. If you leave them in the bag for a few weeks, they hatch right in there, come hopping out, and you've lost the battle! In buggy climates, too, vacuumed-up bug bodies and little lizards and the like can ferment pretty fast in the bag and cause odors. If you only vacuum in one big wall-to-wall campaign once a week, I'd empty the bag with each vacuuming, whether it's full or not. If you're vacuuming daily, I'd dump it weekly.

Your vacuum has a little light that **tells** you when to empty the bag, you say? It may be better than relying on vacuumers ever to remember— but for the most part these electric consciences are not 100 percent reliable.

A too-full bag not only cuts your vacuum's efficiency; it overworks the motor and overworks you, too, because it takes more passes to pick up the dirt. It'll also make a much nastier job of pawing through the bag innards to rescue that earring back or one-of-a-kind washer you just slurped up. And don't be tempted to overfill the disposable paper bags either, trying to pinch pennies. They reduce your vacuum's effectiveness just as fast as they fill and should be discarded when no more than half full. And never attempt to empty and reuse disposable bags. The all-important pores that let the air flow back out of the bag get too plugged up to be efficient after one use.

As for bag emptying technique, even with disposable bags it's a good idea to remember that it isn't "in the bag" till you get it out of the machine and neatly transported to the trash container. If your disposable bags are self-sealing its a cinch, but otherwise hold it upright and with care till you actually get there.

Upend a **cloth** bag very gently onto widely spread newspapers (outside, if at all possible), then stand on the bag ring and shake and knead the sides of the bag good and hard. You can even do a little suction-to-suction resuscitation from time to time by vacuuming the inside of your upright's cloth bag with the wand of your canister vacuum.

There's even a time to change—yes, change, not empty—the cloth bag on your upright vacuum: when it springs a leak and you find yourself doing a lot of dusting **after** you vacuum. You can confirm your diagnosis of this very common ailment by shining a light around the bag while the vacuum is switched on in a darkened room. All that spewed-out dust will show up bright and clear in the light beam!

Is there anything I ought to know about mirror cleaning ? #45

Mirror, mirror on the wall, takes a little extra care in cleaning, that is all.

The way mirrors are placed and the way we use them, they're sitting ducks for soap and water splatters, flossing and brushing fallout, makeup smears, and hairspray haze. (It's a rough life, resting on the razor's edge of vanity.) That shiny, reflective surface that makes them look so good also makes them look extra bad, as every fingerprint, noseprint, fly-speck, and grain of dust shows double.

We're always wiping mirrors down, but they aren't just one more piece of glass, which is how we tend to treat them. That layer of silver on the back that gives mirrors their magic is pretty vulnerable—to everything from the chemicals in human handprints to the chemicals we use to clean them. The mirror's worst enemy, in fact, is that insidious "black edge," caused by water and harsh cleaning chemicals oxidizing the silver plating on back of the glass. Never use strong alkalis (such as ammonia or heavy-duty cleaners) or acids (such as vinegar) to clean a mirror, and keep water well away from the edge. Flooding the edge with a cleaning solution or letting it stand or puddle there is especially bad. Seepage onto the back like this is the single cause of ruined mirrors. How many mirrors have you seen with a case of black edge—silent testimony to careless cleaning?

The right way to clean mirrors is with an alcohol-based cleaning solution like Windex or the kind you buy at a janitorial-supply store in concentrated form and mix up yourself as you need it. Spray it on in a fine mist—not so energetically that it drips and runs all over. Then wipe the mirror dry immediately, especially along the joints and edges. For mirrors with frames or metal trim, spraying the window cleaning solution into the cloth and not onto the glass is the surest way to keep damaging cleaning solution from running down into the frame and collecting there.

Many of my converts to window washing with a squeegee tell me they squeegee their mirrors, too. This is best saved for large expanses like panels and full-length dressing mirrors. And you never want to squeegee mirror tiles—you'll force water into the cracks and onto the silver backing.

Hairspray speckles on a mirror can be removed with window-washing solution and a nylon scrub pad, but a little undiluted rubbing alcohol will dissolve it much faster.

The curse of the mirror cleaner is lint clinging, which a mirror magnifies, of course. Have you ever seen a cloth or paper towel that didn't leave some lint?) Here's how to cure 95 percent of it:

Wrong

The way we usually clean mirrors, every stop leaves a lint bunch!

Right

Take long, full strokes—this way the lint will only be on the edges—then one last long stroke all around the border will pick up all the dropped lint.

P.S. When you **install** a mirror, be sure to mount it at least one sixteenth of an inch from the wall and well above the backsplash, to assure it some air circulation behind and help keep flying water and cleaning solutions from damaging it.

How do I get a soot stain off the face of my stone fireplace ? #46

The answer to this question depends on what kind of stone or masonry it's made of. You can wash smoke, soot, or stains off from hard, slick materials like polished granite, marble, or glazed brick in minutes. If your fireplace facing is sandstone or porous white brick, getting it off without any "etched in stone" gray spots remaining is a miracle.

Smoke (soot) generally doesn't stain; it just clings there until you squirt some liquid on it in an attempt to clean it. Then the solution dissolves it and drives it into the pores and you do have a stain as stubborn as an India ink blot. So you always want to remove as much of

106

the oily smoke and soot particles as possible before ever using any liquid cleaners on there.

Professionals take a three-step approach here:

1. Thoroughly vacuum the area with a vacuum dusting brush to remove any loose material on the surface.

2. Then go over the surface with a dry sponge—a five-inch-by-seven-inch pad of virgin rubber, available at janitorial-supply stores—or an art gum eraser to remove all surface soil possible.

3. Now you're ready at last to wet-clean. Specialty brick and fireplace cleaners are available, but they're unlikely to be any more effective—and they're a lot less safe—than a strong solution of cold-water laundry detergent (one-half a cup per gallon of warm water). Brush the solution on heavily and quickly blot with a thick, clean towel or sponge to remove the loosened dirt before it's absorbed back into the surface. Applying plenty of solution helps to float the dirt out, so I always lay a couple of big old towels at the base of the wall to absorb the runoff. Brush the solution on again, scrub with a stiff nylon brush, then rinse with a sponge dipped in clear water. Repeat as necessary—often several rounds will be required. In your later applications you can let the solution sit on the surface for a few minutes to help it dissolve the soil. Since drips or runs onto uncleaned surfaces may leave marks, always start at the bottom and work upward.

If the stain is in a place that gets pretty hot it's tougher, because the stain is baked on there. In situations like these a powdered cleanser containing bleach might help. And for small oily spots, an aerosol spot remover like K_2r can be helpful. In any case, you want to avoid using muriatic acid brick cleaners. These are for washing stray splatters of mortar from newly installed brick, and their repeated use can deteriorate and weaken mortar joints. Acid cleaners may or may not be effective on smoke stains, and they can eat skin and clothing as well as the surrounding surfaces. If you decide to resort to one of these for a really recalcitrant stain, be sure to cover up anything you don't want ruined, and wear rubber gloves, goggles, and protective clothing—no kidding. Never use acid on marble or travertine. If all else fails, brick and stone can be sandblasted to remove stains, but it will roughen the surface and the sand ends up everywhere.

The real secret here is to avoid this problem by sealing the surface so smoke stains can't penetrate. Once you get it clean or, far better yet, right at the beginning when it's new, apply one or two coats of nonyellowing acrylic masonry sealer, such as concrete or terrazzo seal from a janitorial-supply store. This will close the pores and make the surface easier to clean and deepen and enrich the color of the brick or stone as well.

Speed in cleaning is possible and even fun, and any of you slow movers who think you can't do a good job in a hurry better think again, because you can. Anything worth doing is worth doing fast! All you have to do is apply a couple of simple principles, and you'll be able to clean not just faster but better and can even brag about it at the next block association meeting.

• **Go watch a pro.** If you want to be a champion at anything (cooking, golf, skiing, or cleaning) then go to the champions and learn what they know—what they use and how they go about it. I have a good working knowledge of at least seven trades now—all from watching and working with the pros. They love to show you what they know and to show off! If you have a cleaning service or professional maid come in, you can watch closely, too, and ask questions to learn the tricks of the trade. You can even pay attention to how **you** speed through the place when company's coming and learn from it.

• **Race the clock** on every job of cleaning and go for the gold! It's challenge that makes life come alive. I do dishes five times faster and better than my wife or daughter because I'm always trying to beat my previous record when I dip those dinner plates in. So see how long it takes you to a chore—and see if you can shave a few minutes off each time you do it. Before long I guarantee you'll be considerably faster than before! The sheer exhilaration of doing anything well will power you up here, too. Find out how fast a fastidious friend finishes a frightful job, then scheme, plan and work to break her best time—you'll forget the work part in your eagerness to excel.

• **Prepare well**—round up the right tools **before** the job begins so you won't have to break your stride to hunt up stuff.

• **Seek new tools and better cleaners constantly.** The right tool—in anything—can make all the difference between clomping along and cutting right through. And keep an eye on your inventory. There's no greater waste of time and a good head of cleaning steam than having to drop everything and run to the store because you've just discovered you're out of paper towels or oven cleaner.

• **Carry all your supplies** right along with you in a pocketed apron or cleaning caddy.

• **Don't take breaks,** sit down, or try to watch TV, study, or visit while you work. Just hit it hard once you get started.

• **Do everything as you go**—don't backtrack.

• **Use both hands**—in dusting, sweeping, and vacuuming and whenever you can. One hand moves stuff out of the way while the other swoops through with the dust cloth, vacuum, etc. When you're wall washing, work with sponge in one hand, towel in the other, etc.

• **Don't be ashamed to do "skip" cleaning**—you don't have to do every square inch every time; if it isn't dirty, don't clean it.

• **Combine jobs whenever you can**—start one thing while you're finishing another, let one thing soak while you clean another, etc.

P.S. If you don't **want** to excel at housecleaning all the efficiency courses in kingdom come won't shift your transmission.

What's the right way
to clean eyeglasses  #48

We all wear glasses these days—for sun, style, image, or intimidation (so we can shake them at people in high-powered corporate meetings) —even if we don't need them to see better. And what, of all we own, do we or others see more of? So we should all know the right way to clean them, and it isn't with your shirttail. At least 75 percent of the snazzy lenses we see life through today are plastic, which means they're nice and light and unbreakable. And susceptible . . . to scratches, especially, which can switch a pair of fashion eyewear from sharp to seedy in no time.

The #1 rule here is never to rub lenses—especially plastic lenses—with anything without washing them first. Scrubbing those little particles of dust and grit guaranteed to be on there around on the surface with a dry wipe is just like taking fine sandpaper to it.

So keep your windows on the world bright and clear and unblemished; you want to *wash* them at least daily. This doesn't mean use household glass cleaners on them. The ones containing ammonia, especially, are too hard on the health of plastic frames and lenses. Instead, slip over to the sink and hold your glasses under lukewarm running water. Stick with warm water, not hot, or the frame could expand enough to pop out a lens. Rinse both sides of the lenses well—just steaming the lenses won't do—you've got to rinse or you're just wetting the soil, not removing it. Then add a drop of dish detergent or hand soap, rub it around gently with your fingertips, and rinse again. If there's skin oil and makeup lodged in tight all round the rims, scrub it out with a soft toothbrush, being careful not to rake the newly loosened grime across the lenses. Don't neglect the nose pads, either, because dirt usually cakes up on there only to be transferred to the lenses later. And if you wash the frames as well while you're at it, it'll remove the salt (from sweat) that accumulates there. This, in case you've ever wondered, is what causes those white patches on temples especially—the salt has soaked in and dried out and roughened up the surface of the plastic. If your frames are already salt-damaged, you can at least disguise it by rubbing in a little Vaseline after the area is clean and dry.

The special glasses cleaning solutions sold by optometrists, which often contain some form of alcohol and an antistatic ingredient, do a fine job, too, of course. But it's still good to flush your lenses off under a sturdy stream of water whenever you can. If you get some hairspray or a glob of bacon grease on your glasses, just dip them in a little clean dishwater and reach down in and rub it off.

Even after you wash your glasses, it makes a difference what you use to wipe them dry. Even the softest tissue is made of wood pulp, so no, you *don't* want to use a tissue on plastic lenses, and it's not such a great idea on glass lenses, either. A clean piece of cotton cloth is a lot less linty, as well as softer. You can also use camera lens cleaning cloths, but never the silicone treated "sight saver" type papers on plastic, especially tinted or reflective lenses. If you're out somewhere and your glasses get dusty and there's no approved wiper in sight, stay away from that shirttail and just **blow** on them.

After your glasses are clean and dry, a little 3-in-One oil in the hinges every once in a while will help keep salt from accumulating and corroding there, too. Don't wear your $135 designer frames when you paint the ceiling. Use latex paint if you have to wear any glasses at all up there and wash it off the minute you step off the ladder.

Aside from keeping them clean, the kindest thing you can do for your glasses is to keep them in the case and the case in an unvarying assigned place when they're not on your nose. They'll be much less likely to get sat on, set upon, stepped on, knocked off, or lost. Case out the case occasionally, too. Not a few glasses gashes are caused by dust, dirt, or worn interior padding in what should be their one safe haven.

What's the best way to get incredibly sticky Ohio (Idaho, North Carolina, Maine, etc.) mud off your shoes and boots

#49

- Stay out of the fields until June.
- Wade through the swimming pool thirty-one times.
- Wear your socks on the outside of your boots.
- Have a local mechanic blast it off with a pressure washer.

These are thoughts and temptations, but not quite the answer for those of us who regularly—or at least occasionally—get muddy boots or shoes.

Rule of thumb #1: Divest! Don't just give your feet a few fast scrapes on the mat or sill and head inside. You can never—I say emphatically—**never** clean a muddy boot or shoe well enough in this manner to pass muster for wearing it into the house. The cleats, waffles, soles, heels, seams, creases, and laces will trap and hold hidden mud, which once dried in the warm house expands two hundred times its original volume into dust. And the ever more elaborately patterned soles of running shoes, etc., will leave oddly shaped little mud chunks everywhere.

Take the boots OFF and leave them outside or just inside the door (or in the mud room, should you be in the enviable position of owning one). If you make sure the mudroom has a bench, muddy household members are much more likely to stop and sit and deboot themselves. You'd better provide a place, too, to receive bemired boots and soil-loaded shoes—they're going to end up somewhere! An old rug or towel, rubber drainboard, or plastic tub will do, though rubber boot trays with a raised lip are available. Or best of all, a rubber-backed nylon or olefin mat of the type pro cleaners use at every building entrance to stop foot traffic trompings right in their tracks. These mats are long-lasting and good-looking and catch rain and snow drippings as well as mud and gravel.

Rule #2: Banish bare dirt in the dooryard! It'll at least minimize the mud that makes it in if there's **some** form of paving or grass at least five steps before the entrance. Sidewalk, driveway, brick, concrete, asphalt— even a row of flagstones—will give feet a chance to dry out and walk some of it off before they hit the threshold.

Rule #3: Consider a foot scraper. I'm always in favor of a synthetic turf mat outside exterior doorways, but mud calls for even more serious measures. A foot scraper off to the side of the steps will help—and the sturdier the better, whether it's a metal mesh mat or an upright metal blade. Blade scrapers with built-in brushes are better even if the brushes do clog pretty quick, because scrapers in general seem to slight the fact that as much can accumulate on the sides as on the bottom.

Rule #4. Smoother soles are better. Deeply indented soles such as Vibram do a lot for an outdoorsy image, but you don't have to be a janitor long to learn to hate them. They make black marks all over and are about perfectly designed for mud and animal manure pickup. They chew up lawns and grounds and trails, too—if you don't climb mountains carrying sixty-pound packs you really don't need them. Get yourself a nice, new pair of smooth soled chukkas and see how much easier mud cleanup can be.

Rule #5. Think before you set foot in it. Don't just tell yourself you won't get muddy this time. Check out the conditions out there and arm your feet accordingly. Why do you think the Lord made rubber boots and galoshes?

Rule #6: Get it off before it dries. Admittedly we never feel like facing it right then, when we've just come in out of the wet and muck and maybe cold, too. But letting all that glop dry on there only makes things harder. Then we have to scrape and chisel it off—no favor to fine cowhide—and rewet everything to remove the remaining traces anyway.

So get it while it's fresh and get it over with—outdoors, if weather permits and if at all possible. If you have to do this indoors, hold the shoe or boot over a waste container and get off all you can with a putty knife or large screwdriver. Wipe off as much as possible of the rest with a damp cloth or paper towel. Then scrub off whatever's left with a soft brush under a running faucet, working as quickly as you can to keep down water penetration. Blot dry immediately with a cloth or paper towel and let the shoes or boots dry the rest of the way themselves. Then you can retreat with leather conditioner.

P.S. If all else fails, you can put them back on the next day— warm or dry or wet—and walk it off!

Are those concentrated cleaners as easy to use as the pre-mixed—how careful do I have to be in diluting them ? ○ #50

A stronger brew counts for a lot in a Kentucky still operation, but in cleaning too much can mean too bad! More is better when you're weighing gold, but not necessarily so in cleaning. Just because a teaspoon of baking powder makes the biscuits rise, would we put in a cup of the stuff to really make 'em fluff up? Overdosing doesn't make any more sense in cleaning. The proper dilution is as important in cleaning as it is in cooking; a teaspoon of salt better be a teaspoon of salt, or the soup is ruined.

We professionals often use Joy, the dishwashing liquid, for our window squeegeeing solution, for example. For this purpose you need just ten drops in a gallon of water. This amount of detergent makes the water wetter so it will "sheet out" on the glass, lubricates the squeegee so it glides smoothly, and provides a gentle, emulsifying action to loosen soil. A long squirt of the very same detergent will foam the water and streak the window and leave a sticky residue.

Yet we so often think that when we **really** want to clean we should put **more** of the cleaner in and make the solution stronger. But a too-strong cleaning solution actually does a poorer job in most cases. Too much chemical affects the water's ability to suspend dirt particles in the solution and flush them away. An overly powerful cleaning solution can also damage delicate surfaces and dry out and irritate the skin on your hands, as well as cost more than it needs to and cause a lot of unnecessary extra rinsing.

The big secret is to actually read what it says on the label about dilution and then **measure** the chemical out—don't just glug and guess. The reason we so often get in trouble here is that we all pride ourselves on our "eye"—but is that unerring eyeball actually ever put to the test? I hold an Accurate Mix contest at many of my professional cleaners' seminars, giving each contestant a bottle of cleaner and telling him to pour what he thinks is three ounces into a bucket. These are professionals with a lot more practice than you and they always average two and a half times **more** than is needed! If the pros can't judge three ounces accurately by eye, chances are you can't either.

So if it says sixteen-to-one dilution, measure out one cup of concentrate and add sixteen cups of water (one gallon). Sixty to one, a common dilution, means half a cup of cleaner to two gallons of water. Pay attention to the water part, too. Do you even know the exact size of the bucket you usually mix your cleaning solutions in? Are you mixing up that brew in a big sink, a little sink, a laundry tub, a mini bucket, and a maxi bucket, or what? Again don't guess—measure.

I'll confess that even we pros wrinkle our brows over the matter of proper mixing—so we have a shortcut called premeasured cleaners. Yes, that means concentrate already doled out into neat little plastic envelopes that contain precisely the right amount to make a certain volume of cleaning solution. You just snip off the corner and pour into your spray bottle or bucket of water. This makes it neat and convenient and easy to store cleaning supplies even in several different cleaning stations around the house. The premeasured pouches available in janitorial-supply stores from PortionPac and others are even color coded (different colors for all-purpose, heavy-duty, and disinfectant cleaners, for example) as further insurance against human error.

P.S. Always put the cleaning chemical into the water, not vice versa, **especially** with acid cleaners. *Pouring* water into a puddle of concentrated cleaner can splash it into your eyes or onto nearby surfaces.

How do I clean a textured ceiling or wall ? #51

When people ask me, "How do I clean my textured surfaces?" I know in my heart that they're not referring to tasteful light texturing, but to the half-inch stalactite job some "craftsman" applied to hide his ceiling cracks or sheet rock seams. A surface like this is as challenging and craggy as the Rocky Mountains, and it's usually blessed with only a single coat of cheap latex paint. No one could clean this combination.

When you're up against a case of unrealistic texturing the only sane course is to level it a little and paint it. Extremely deep, craggy textures can be scrubbed with a brush and flood-rinsed, but that's an awful lot of trouble. I think it makes a lot more sense to tame down the texture to something manageable by removing all those sharp points that snag cleaning clothes and sponges.

You can do this by dragging a flat board across the surface, pressing hard enough to knock off the tips of the little pinnacles. A light sanding may then be necessary to smooth up sharp edges. Then a couple of good coats of washable semigloss enamel applied with a long-nap roller will fill in and level a lot of the remaining roughness, making future cleaning much more faceable.

As for decent texture, I love to clean it; you can clean it so quickly and easily and it sure hides the streaks. You do it the same as any wall, using the two-bucket system, of course (see p. 21). Just be sure to use a cellulose sponge rather than a rag that will catch in the crevices. You also need to apply the cleaning solution (all-purpose cleaner or degreaser solution if the surface is greasy) more generously than usual to float the soil out of all those little valleys and canyons. Leave the liquid on there a couple of minutes to emulsify the soil and then dry and polish with a clean terry towel, blotting deep indentations well to be sure to remove every last bit of the cleaning solution.

Are there places in a home that really NEED disinfecting ❓ #52

The more TV we watch, the surer we are that toilet trolls and grout gremlins lurk in every crack and corner and will "get us" if we don't douse them with some kind of deadly antibacteria broth. But we have to remember that germs—bacteria, viruses, fungi, etc.—are everywhere, and only a certain number of them make us any mischief. Many of them are beneficial. And simple cleanliness will do as much—or more—to get rid of germs than any germ-killing chemical.

In a home situation there's no such thing as getting all the little buggers anyway—the best we can do is reduce their numbers. We can't "sterilize" the bathroom or the baby's bassinet—sterile is what operating rooms and surgical instruments are, and it's a costly and exacting procedure. What we're really doing when we apply a disinfectant at home is sanitizing—cutting the germ population way down periodically to help keep possibly hazardous organisms under control. A disinfectant solution used properly will kill all of the living germs of some types, but not all types are susceptible, and dormant spores will still be left in any case. It wouldn't make sense to try to kill all the germs in the whole house, even if it were possible. Every time the door opened or someone sneezed, we'd have to start all over.

There are places in the home where reducing the germ population makes sense: 1) to eliminate odors, which are a byproduct of bacterial growth, 2) to help prevent mildew, which is a form of fungus, (see p. 166; and 3) to help prevent the spread of disease. What are the target areas?

For control of odors and mildew as well as germs:

toilet bowls, sinks, and other bathroom surfaces

tub and shower areas

diaper pails

garbage cans and garbage disposals

pet living areas and anything that comes in frequent contact with pet wastes

For control of contagious diseases:

doorknobs, faucets, and banisters

light switches and heavily used cabinet handles

telephone receivers

sickroom surfaces, linens, and eating utensils

And to be sure you're disinfecting, not just wetting, whatever you lay sponge to:

• Don't casually mix disinfectants with other cleaners. Many soaps and detergents react chemically with disinfectants and seriously affect the disinfectant's ability to do its thing.

• Clean the area well before disinfecting. Dirt—especially the "organic soils" that abound in the kinds of places we like to disinfect— will also weaken the action of most disinfectants.

• Don't forget the cracks and crevices—germ heaven.

• If you're really serious about disinfecting, leave the solution on the surface for at least five and preferably ten minutes before you wipe or rinse it away.

• Change the water, your disinfecting solution, as soon as it starts to get dingy, or you'll just be moving bugs around, not removing them.

If this all seems like a lot of effort, think how good you'll feel after you've waged your germ warfare and emerged victorious!

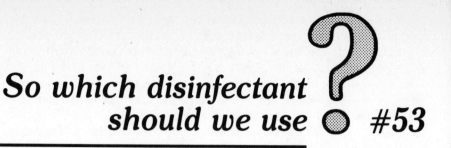

So which disinfectant should we use ? #53

Disinfectants are such strong and potentially dangerous chemicals that the search for a better—safer and more effective—one never stops. Not long ago the phenolic disinfectants, made from carbolic acid, were among the most widely used. Remember the original formula Lysol? They're good germ killers, all right, but even the newer synthetic phenols are fairly toxic to humans and animals, especially cats. They're also hard on the skin, have an unmistakable disinfectant odor, and tend to corrode chrome and other metals. So if the list of active ingredients on the label includes the terms "phenol" or "phenyl," I'd leave it on the shelf. Don't worry if a label says "phenol coefficient," though; that's just a measure of the product's germ-killing ability, measured against what phenolics can do.

Liquid chlorine bleach is another powerful and fast-working disinfectant, but its ability to weaken fibers, rust metal, dull finishes, and remove color doesn't exactly recommend it for wholesale use around the home. I would use a bleach/water solution (a half to one cup of bleach per quart of water) to kill mildew on tub and shower tile grout—it's much better and cheaper for the purpose than anything else. Just be sure you rinse it afterward with clear water to avoid damaging the grout. Aside from that, I'd keep bleach confined to the laundry.

Pine oil is also a pretty good sanitizer in strong enough concentrations, if at least 20 percent of the cleaner in question actually is pine oil, and many people like pine cleaners for that "fresh, clean smell" they leave behind. Many pine cleaners don't contain enough pine oil to actually disinfect, though, and since pine oil doesn't work on as wide a range of bacteria pine preparations are often beefed up with other chemicals. Check the label.

An excellent and very safe disinfectant that's effective against a wider range of microorganisms than most is the one used by many animal handlers. It goes by the trade name of Nolvasan or Chlorasan and especially if you're regularly disinfecting pet areas or accessories, it would be worth the trouble to run some down. Many vets carry it.

The all-around disinfectant I like best for home use is the quaternary type. You can tell a "quat," too, by reading the label: the active ingredient will be listed as some form of ammonium chloride. Quats combine well with soaps and detergents for good cleaning action—some even come with a detergent built right in, so you can have a dual-purpose "disinfectant cleaner." Quats are easier on household surfaces, and they're safer for us to use and handle, too. You can get quat disinfectants in concentrated form from a janitorial-supply store at very reasonable prices or buy them ready-to-use at the supermarket by such names as Lysol Deodorizing Cleaner and Dow Bathroom Cleaner.

Whichever one you decide to go with; remember that though their intended targets may be small, disinfectants were designed to **kill** things. So avoid breathing disinfectant sprays or mist for any length of time; keep disinfectants well away from your eyes and mouth and strictly out of the reach of children and pets. And read and **follow** the instructions on the label. If you show sensitivity to a product, stop using it immediately.

My PC is dirty now; how can I spruce it up without messing it up **?** **#54**

Well, you could try typing upside down for a couple of days—just kidding!

It's actually pretty important to keep your computer clean, but whatever you see on the outside of it is the least of your problems. A gummy keyboard and obscured CRT screen may be a bit of a nuisance, but the real killers are the dust, lint, and smoke particles that may have found their way inside. The hot gadgets inside your computer are like magnets for dust. And that dust and dirt, cat hair, whatever—gets sucked into the machine and acts like a blanket and makes the components even hotter so they fail long before they should.

An accumulation of dust on the disk drive head can damage disks, destroy data, and affect the drive's ability to read and write information. At least 50 percent of all disk drive crashes are due simply to drive mechanics getting dirty and gummed up. You don't have to lug your PC down to a technician to get the heads cleaned; you can do it yourself right at home. It's as easy as popping in a head cleaning disk from the computer store and letting it run, so this is definitely a piece of preventive maintenance you should get in the habit of performing several times a year. It can save you a lot of expense and frustration down the road.

Another unquestionably worthwhile idea is to *keep the stuff from getting in there in the first place.* I realize this means the kinds of fussy, boring, wet-blanket things we never like to be bothered with, but I'm going to say them anyway—put a dust cover on your machine when you're not using it and store your disks in their jackets in a covered holder. Don't smoke, eat, or drink around your computer and try to keep its surroundings as dust-free as you can.

Before cleaning your computer's housing, unplug the machine and vacuum out any ventilation grilles or holes. Don't use solvents, abrasives, or other harsh cleaners on the plastic case. There are special antistatic cleaning solutions and wipes available for computers, or you can use what the techs use, just plain alcohol or alcohol-based window cleaner. The secret is simply making sure no liquid gets inside the case—water is the kiss of death for anything electronic, which is why you don't want to be constantly nursing a cold or hot drink right next to one. Use just a slightly damp cloth to gently wipe the surface of the machine; never spray cleaner directly onto the case or use a soppy sponge or cloth, which could drip inside. Be careful around any openings in the case, such as disk drive slots or switch holes, and don't get liquid on any of the connectors.

Because of its static charge the CRT screen attracts more than its share of airborne particles. It should be dusted regularly with an antistatic dust cloth and wiped with alcohol to remove smudges.

With all the oils, lotions, and sticky stuff on our hands, keyboards can get pretty gunky. A clean keyboard not only looks sharp, but works better, too. So remove any dust with a vacuum brush attachment, then key by key gently wipe off the oily soils. You don't want to use any water here, either, so reach for the alcohol again or the special keyboard cleaning wipes available from computer dealers. Alcohol can also be used on a cotton swab to reach tight places.

Some computer stores have complete kits for maintaining your PC. These usually include antistat dust cloths, a head cleaning kit, antistat case and screen cleaners, and a keyboard cleaning solution. There are also cans of pressurized air for dusting hard-to-reach places, antistatic cleaners for the whole area surrounding the computer, antistatic floor mats to set under your feet, and even custom-designed swabs for every imaginable computer orifice and cranny. All of this is meritorious and convenient, but you don't absolutely have to have special "computer" cleaning products for anything but the head cleaning. The fabric softening sheets used in the laundry room, for example, make a fine antistatic dust cloth and general wipe for computers, once they've been through the dryer.

P.S. Before long computers will surely be smart enough to assess their own condition and inform us accordingly:

"Clean me now."
"Bad job—do it again."
"Oh oh—better call a pro!"

How should I clean Plexiglas, Lucite, Lexan, and other clear plastics ? ○ #55

Slowly, carefully, and not too often! The glass in our homes is hard to hurt in the process of cleaning, and we tend to think of Plexiglas in the same way. After all, they look so much alike and they're used for so many of the same purposes. We're always somehow surprised to discover that Plexiglas isn't glass, it's a soft, flexible acrylic plastic. Ammonia, most acids, and many solvents, including nail polish remover and lacquer thinner, can melt or cloud it, and even our old faithful alcohol-based window cleaners (Windex) may damage it. Hot water isn't good for its health either, and powdered cleansers, including the softest, will scratch it. Scraping it with a knife or razor blade will make a permanent

127

record of each stroke, and a mean look on your worst day might even mark it! Then why do we even use it?

It's super safe. You'll find it on storm doors and windows and other breakable places that need visibility and light, but get more than their share of the wrath of the elements and the occupants.

It's cheap. Since 1979, building codes have required nonbreakable material in doors and for windows next to doors or near the floor. Safety glass is thick, heavy, and expensive. Plexiglas is thinner, lighter, less costly, and easier to install.

Many people who get Plexiglas end up unhappy with it because it scratches so easily, but it's durable as well as practical as long as it's cared for properly.

As for the right way to clean Plexiglas, the manufacturers recommend the special Plexiglas cleaners found at any glass store. Most Plexiglas cleaners are creamy polishes that not only clean but also leave a protective antistatic coating on the plastic. Some contain waxes that improve the clarity and appearance of the Plexi by filling and bridging small scratches. A mild, neutral detergent also can be used to clean it, but this does nothing to condition the plastic or smooth or cover scratches.

Before applying any cleaner to Plexiglas, flood-rinse it well with clean water. This will remove the dust particles sure to be on there, which will scratch and dull the surface if rubbed around on it. For this same reason you **never** want to wipe dirty Plexi with a dry cloth. And even when wiping with a cloth wet with cleaning solution, wipe gently in a circular motion, because circular scratches show up less! Don't drag and rub the cloth against the plastic—wipe a short ways, then lift and switch to a clean section of the cloth and wipe a short ways more. I keep saying "cloth" here because a soft, clean cotton cloth is much safer for Plexiglas than a possibly hard-surfaced paper towel. And if you're cleaning along and run into a hunk of bird dirt—which usually contains undigestible sand or seeds—any scrubbing or polishing will scratch that window for sure.

A squeegee can be used to clean Plexiglas if handled gently, but if you get a bit of grit caught under the blade and pull it across the Plexi, you'll be sorry. So again rinse well first and apply lots of solution to float off what you can. Let it sit on there a couple of seconds and then gently squeegee it off, letting the water and any debris float ahead of the blade. Don't let the window get dry halfway through!

For five-hundred-dollar airplane or limousine windshields, it makes sense to buff out scratches with the kits available that enable you to work your way from coarse to the finest of grits and then a series of polishes and buffings to restore the Plexi to apparent perfection, but it takes an amazing amount of energy and determination. For storm doors and windows at home, it's faster and cheaper to just replace the Plexi when it gets bad.

What about those pine cleaners—do they do anything besides smell good ❓ *#56*

Not everyone would say they smell good, for starters. The scent of pine cleaner reminds one person of a fresh forest breeze, another may think it makes a house more "hospital" than hospitable. Remember the first rule about odor: it's organic soils and bacteria that cause it. If you clean well and use a disinfectant cleaner in especially odor-prone areas, you won't need floral deodorizers hanging from your towel bar or strong-scented cleaning solutions to keep things smelling good.

Many people like an aroma that convinces them they're cleaning, though, so manufacturers obligingly add lemon, mint, or sassafras scent to their detergent formulations for this very reason. In the case of true pine oil cleaners, though, the aroma is natural. Pine oil, distilled from pine trees, is one of the important active cleaning ingredients in these products, and you get the scent as a bonus. Pine oil is a solvent that penetrates and dissolves oils and tars, which is why you shouldn't use it straight or leave it long on surfaces you don't want to remove the paint or wax from. In strong enough concentrations, pine oil is also a pretty good germicide, and one of the appeals of pine cleaners is their ability to clean, degerm, and deodorize all in one pass. To be effective as a sanitizer a product should contain at least 20 percent pine oil, such as Pine-Sol—check the labels.

There's a *coneful* of pine oil products on the market, and their effectiveness varies from brand to brand, but the better ones, such as Pine-Sol, Pine Power, and Spic and Span Pine, are excellent all-purpose cleaners. If you want a good all-around cleaner that also deodorizes and sanitizes (see p. 120 for the difference between this and disinfection) . . . if you're not allergic to aromatic piney or resinous fragrances . . . and if you want to be sure everyone knows you just spruced up the bathroom—go for it!

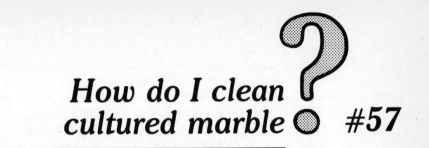

How do I clean cultured marble ● #57

With nothing harsh or abrasive, for sure. We're under the impression that "'marbled"' means immortal—hard, indestructible, forever! But that's not true. Marble itself is one of the softest of building stones—it has a hardness of 2.8–3.00, as the scientists like to express it. That's not much harder than a human fingernail, so marble is actually very easily scratched. Real marble also chips, stains, and oxidizes readily, acids eat it for breakfast, and alkalis and strong alkaline cleaners yellow it. So you can

131

see why man-made or cultured marble was invented—a colorful veined and swirled surface that doesn't need as much coddling. The marble-looking one-piece vanity tops that have the sink molded right in are cast of cultured marble, as are many flat vanity and counter tops with separate sinks and even some tubs and tub enclosures. Cultured marble is made from a mixture of marble dust and plastic resins, and it's denser than real marble so it's more resistant to staining. But cultured marble will lose its luster and start looking old fast if you punish it at cleaning time. So do it right—clean it with a spray bottle of disinfectant cleaner and a soft cloth. The only heavy cleaning artillery I'd use is a white-backed nylon sponge. And **keep it wet while you're working with it!** Never use powdered cleanser, steel wool, metal scrubbers, or colored scrub pads on cultured marble, or you'll scratch and mar the surface. As a last resort, you could use one of the "soft scrub" type cleaners or a paste of baking soda and water, but even then go easy— don't rub hard and never bear down on it.

Cultured marble may not stain much, but it will dull, and if that happens it can be brought back with a polishing compound such as the kind used to revitalize vehicle finishes. Burns or deep scratches or small cuts can be sanded out with increasingly finer grades of sandpaper and finished up with polishing compound.

A regular coating, after you clean it, with a clear resin type product like Gel Gloss, appliance wax, or a furniture polish like Pledge or Jubilee will fill hairline scratches and give your cultured marble a nice cultured pearly glow.

Does it matter whether the cleaning solution is hot or cold ❓ #58

The hotter the water, the faster those little water molecules move around and the more aggressive they get. Remember learning about that back in chemistry class? Hence hot water usually breaks down dirt better and faster. Heat helps a lot, too, when you're trying to remove heavy layers of grease or wax or rinse your way to spotless stemware. And in things like dish washing and disinfecting, warm-as-possible water is the only way to get maximum germ kill. Warmer water also dissolves

133

soap or detergent faster and is just plain more pleasant to dip your hands into.

Getting the solution hot enough to burn the hair off your hands, however, is kind of futile, because very soon after the solution is spread out on the floor, wall, window, or whatever it drops right down to room temperature. So it isn't worth getting all steamed up about. It's more important to use the right cleaner, to dilute it properly, and to give it time to work and emulsify the soil. Hotter water emulsifies faster, if it would only stay hot long enough. For most general cleaning, you might as well use agreeably warm water.

In a controlled-environment chore like laundry, though, where a steaming-hot tub of water isn't significantly cooled by a batch of clothes, a hot-water wash can be a real help for heavily soiled or greasy loads. Liquid bleach loses its effectiveness rapidly in cooler water, so most bleached white loads are done hot or at least warm. Warm water will do just fine for most other wash, and all-fabric bleaches work o.k. in warm water. A cold wash is usually reserved for dark or bright colors that tend to bleed, loads with blood or protein stains, or special care fabrics whose labels come right out and call for a cold wash.

When washing in cold water do be sure to use a special cold water detergent, because regular laundry products just can't cut it in cold water. A cold rinse, on the other hand, is nearly always a good idea—it not only saves energy but minimizes wrinkling of permanent press fabrics.

Whenever you're doing any cleaning where the instructions call for "cool" or "cold" water, bear in mind that cold, for cleaning purposes, means not ice-cube cold but "not much below eighty degrees." A forty-or fifty-degree solution loses a lot of its cleaning power—it's too numb to work!

Before I leave you with the notion that hotter is always better, let me mention at least three times it's not:

• You never want to use hot water on wood or cork.

• Heat sets most stains, so stained clothing should never be washed warm or hot, dried with heat, or ironed before the stain is removed.

• In the process of carpet shampooing, you do want a good hot extraction solution to be sure all the embedded soil will be emulsified and floated away. But don't let it get over 140° on the newer generations of stain-resistant carpeting, or you'll lose some of those stain-repelling properties.

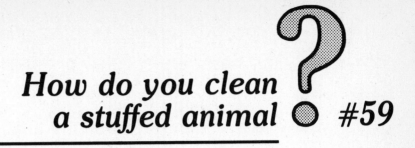

How do you clean **?**
a stuffed animal ● *#59*

I'm sure you mean the kind we cuddle up with, not the kind we peer through a museum case to see. They do get pretty dingy, though Kodiak bear brown and gorilla gray may not show the slow accumulation for a while. Because you never know what the stuffing might be, you'd better not toss your fleecy friend into the washing machine or soak him.

Risk the washer only if the label on the critter clearly says so, which will often mean it has acrylic fur and 100 percent polyester filling, for instance. The "infant" lines of stuffed toys are often washer safe, for example. Among the things that will never emerge from the top loader looking the same as they went in are: very long-furred, shaggy pets, pets with airbrushing (dye sprayed over the fur to make those sprightly little stripes and highlights), pets with flocked noses or lots of glued-on felt features, pets stuffed with foam rubber, paper, or nutshells (yes, nut-

135

shells), and pets with music or voice boxes inside or little tennis rackets or grand pianos attached. And anything you bring home from an amusement park or fair.

Even if the tag says so and it passes the above tests, check the creature over for about-to-burst seams and stains that need pretreating. Then tuck him into a mesh bag and give him a couple of towels or other soft washables to help balance the load and pad his journeys past the agitator. Don't use anything except a gentle or delicate wash cycle. Add an enzyme detergent and perhaps a little powdered bleach if you have a polar bear or piglet with a bad case of the yellows.

To dry, use the stationary sweater drying rack in your dryer or set him somewhere in the sun to air dry. Then sit him in your lap and comb or brush him back to becoming.

Surface clean the method to use for the rest of your unwashable zoo. If the animal is really dirty, vacuum all dust and clinging debris from the fur first. A cordless vac comes in handy here. Then in a bowl or bucket work up a lather of carpet and upholstery cleaner or Woolite and water. Sponge a light amount of suds only on the soiled areas and then wipe it off with a towel. Use another sponge dampened in plain water to rinse, so the animal won't dry all sticky and soapy. You never want to flood the animal with the solution; use as little as possible. If you wet your pet too much, the biggest share of the dirt will just be wicked down into the roots of the fur and the body of the bear. As soon as you're done washing, dry immediately with a clean towel, always wiping with the nap. If you have a wet/dry vacuum, you could use it to suck the fabric free of all the shampoo foam and moisture you can. Set the animal in a place with good air circulation for a day or two afterward to make sure it dries completely and get rid of any lingering chemical odors or "wet pet" smell. Then you can carefully brush, comb, and fluff that little pelt back to luxurious.

P.S. If you have a pedigreed pet of real fur and/or genuine leather, this is a case for the dry cleaners. Never give a freshly dry cleaned pet to a child till the chemical fumes have a chance to air away, but then that's probably not who the mink teddy belongs to anyway.

Is vinegar a good cleaner  #60

Sorry, all you sour apple enthusiasts, tradition and that seductive squeak have misled you. Vinegar isn't a cleaner, it's a mild acid, and if you mix it with water it makes a mildly acid solution. A cleaner is designed to break down dirt and grease and keep them afloat in the cleaning solution, so they can be spirited away. Vinegar won't cut grease or dissolve soil on floors, walls, or windows nearly as well as a true detergent will.

There's a little matter of "pH" involved here, too. Since 85 percent of our common household soils such as oils, fats, and greases are acidic,

137

we use alkaline cleaners to attack them. Acid liquids such as vinegar are only effective on alkaline soils, such as hard water scale.

Vinegar does play an important part as a pH balancer in many stain removal procedures, and it has real value as a **rinsing** agent—it does a good job of neutralizing the soap residue left when you're cleaning floors or washing clothes. Most detergents are alkaline and they leave an alkaline residue, so a vinegar solution (half a cup of white vinegar to a gallon of water for floors, an eighth of a cup to a washer load, and 50/50 white vinegar/water for spotting) is great for the final mop, rinse, or flush. It'll make the floor look brighter and take its new coat of wax better and bring the colors of your laundry back to life. But too many people, following the directions of unknowing floor salesmen, have tried to totally maintain a kitchen floor with vinegar and water. Then they wonder why the chairs have been sticking to the floor lately.

Vinegar is also good for brightening stained aluminum cookware, removing tarnish from copper and brass, and dissolving hard water spots on dishes and glassware. A good vinegar soak will work wonders for clouded drinking glasses or scaly teakettles or coffeepots. And a run-through of 50/50 vinegar/water solution will do a lot to decongest plugged-up coffeemakers or steam irons. For heavy-duty lime removal such as shower heads, shower doors, bathroom fixtures, and exterior windows, however, a good strong phosphoric acid cleaner (see p. 67) will be much faster and more effective than vinegar. Vinegar, like its frequent home remedy companion baking soda, does have some deodorizing qualities, too. You can use a pot of boiling vinegar and water to chase cabbage, fish, or onion odors away or a plain old bowl of vinegar and water to help reclaim the atmosphere of a smoke-filled room. It can help sweeten drains and garbage disposals and thermos bottles and refrigerator innards, too. No matter how many earnest people tell you so, however, it is **not** up to obliterating all the odor from pet accidents (see p. 68 for something that *will* do it.)

How can I make my house look good in a hurry #61

The phone rings, and it's Mike and Marsha; they just happen to be driving through. She was Immaculate Homemaker of the Year last year, and he's dean of organizational science at Georgia Tech. They co-host a radio talk show that tells all. You have ten minutes, max, before they "drop by."

This happens to every one of us, and we all dread it. Don't panic and don't just shovel the bulk of the junk quickly into the nearest closet.

1. First **turn up all the lights!** Yes, brighter not dimmer helps a dirty house look clean. There's a tendency to try to hide cobwebs, dust, and dropped popcorn by subduing the light, but the opposite is true. Darkness causes shadows, mystery, suspicion. Your place, even clean, will give guests a "cover up" feeling if it's darkened. Brightly lit homes feel good and visitors feel better and they'll remember that nice feeling and forget the sweat sock or dog bone sticking out from under the sofa.

2. Then **clean yourself up**—a little makeup or quick shave, new shirt or blouse or sweater. A quick upgrade of **your** appearance goes a long way toward making things seem under control—after all, they'll be seeing a lot more of you than they will of the house.

3. **Enlist all the help you can, quick**—but don't force or threaten anyone into it—they're likely to retaliate by saying something to the guest like, "Boy, if you don't believe in resurrection, you should have seen this place fifteen minutes ago."

4. How small a part of the house can you **confine** them to?—it'll help a lot if you can target your efforts. If it's at least 60 degrees, you can stay on the porch or deck or terrace, outside. Otherwise stick with the living room or kitchen or at least the lower story. Close all the other doors and decide now what you're going to say when they ask for the grand tour of the house—and the kid with the messiest bedroom acts like he's going to take them up on it.

5. **Cast your eye over the entrance area**—porch, door, entryway, steps, even the sidewalk leading up to it. This is what gives that fatal first impression and sets the tone for the whole abode. Remove any out-of-season ornaments and anything crooked or rusty and scoop up all those chewed bones, broken toys, muddy boots, dirty doormats, grubby pet dishes, dead plants, and half-composted shopping flyers.

6. **Dejunk**—especially any empty food containers, strewn clothes, garbage, etc. Merely removing all the loose litter and rearranging everything out of place will do wonders. But *do* leave reading material and half-done projects out. They make you look industrious and intellectual and will give the guest a complex that will help keep his mind off the "wash me" etched in the dust on the TV screen. If nothing's out there already, spread your one-quarter-done quilt, the first draft of the family history, some seed catalogs, or the kids' salt-dough diorama of the moon out in the middle of the living room floor—"in progress" excuses the most unimaginable messes.

7. **Hide the dog and cat.** If they don't see an animal they never look for animal mess.

8. **Floors** play a big part in an overall aura of cleanliness. So do squander a few minutes sweeping or vacuuming. If you're really rushed, you don't even have to haul out the vacuum—just hand-pick all the obvious stuff off the carpet.

9. Next **hit the mirrors** and glass doors and any picture windows or glass furniture tops within the target area. They look so good when

they're sparkling clean and so bad when they're even slightly streaked, handprinted, or spotted. You get a lot of mileage from a quick glass cleaning.

10. If you don't have a dishwasher to stash undone dishes in, pile them in a sinkful of sudsy water. You can also **leave a vacuum, dust cloth, and maybe a bottle of furniture polish out in plain sight.** Explain at some length when they first arrive how you were just in the middle of the weekly cleaning.

11. Run in the kitchen and prepare a **fresh drink of lemonade in your prettiest pitcher.** They'll notice it more than anything else— just don't feed or refresh them too much or they'll have to use the bathroom. The bathroom, by the way, is the next place to hit quickly, if there's still time. Pull the shower curtain shut; hit the sink, faucets, toilet; neaten up the towels. Even if they don't use it, the relaxation will show in your facial muscles and you'll be a better hostess.

Whatever you do, don't **apologize for the condition of the house.** When they ask how are things, take a deep breath and say, "We've been rather busy between our jobs, our exercise program, our night classes at the college, and church and scout leadership activities, and the time we like to devote to volunteer trail building, historic landmark preservation, and voter registration. Plus we had to take a few extra hours out to make hot meals for all our neighbors. We haven't used the living room for weeks, but we're really glad you happened by at the same time." Be sure to find the TV knob and get the set turned off before you launch into this.

Is there anything on an air conditioner that ought to be cleaned ? ● #62

Indeed, and the experts say it cuts energy costs 10 to 15 percent if you just remember to do it—now that's a bit of a surprise to the best of us. What's there in an air conditioner that needs cleaning? There's the outside of the cabinet, of course, which we might actually give a thought to from time to time, and at least two internal parts, in an **unplugged** air conditioner, that need attention, the filter and the coils. Remember that air, which is full of dust, circulates constantly through the filters and coils

142

of both portable and central air conditioners. When the filter is filled and clogged with debris, the fan has to work harder to circulate the air, so it uses more electricity to give you less cooling. Some models have washable foam filters and some the replaceable type. Monthly cleaning or replacement during the air conditioning season will pay big dividends. And air conditioner filters are as inexpensive as that other neglected species, furnace filters.

To clean your filter, prepare a sinkful of disinfectant cleaner solution (air conditioner filters pick up a lot of floating mold and mildew spores) and wash the foam square gently in it. Then rinse it just as gently and put it back in place. And **don't** run the air conditioner till it is back in place. Wipe off the fan blades, too, while you're at it and check your owner's manual to see where the drain holes are and make sure they're not stopped up.

The coils or metal heat-exchanger "fins" that the air passes through to cool it will also get matted with lint, pet hair, etc., over time. By fall these can be packed so tight with debris that when you turn the unit on again in spring only hot air will come out. Gently vacuum the fins out when you clean the filter, but be careful not to bend the fins or cut yourself on those sharp edges.

Air conditioner mechanics and dealers have some real horror stories about full coils, and guess what one of the biggies is for indoor units—tar and nicotine from cigarette smoke. If this is your situation spray on a strong solution of ammonia and clean them off.

Outside AC compressors fill with things like leaves and pine needles and need to be cleaned out every so often, too.

The real challenge with room air conditioners is keeping those fiendish little louvers and grilles degrimed. If they're removable, scrub them in the sink with a stiff brush and warm, soapy water—no, soaking alone won't do it—then rinse and dry. If they're firmly locked in place, heave a sigh and swab them out with a cleaning cloth wrapped around a putty knife.

P.S. If you want really clean air in your home, there are better filters for your central heating/cooling system than the inexpensive fiberglass or oil-treated ones. I'm talking about electrostatic filters. These set up an electric charge that "magnetizes" the dirt particles in the air that's passed through them so that all the dirt is attracted to a collection grid. An electrostatic filter costs four to six hundred dollars or so, but it'll last almost forever.

How could my cleaning tool be dirtier than what I'm cleaning ❓ ⭕ #63

Let's just take a tour of the cleaning rags and tools at home—I'm afraid we'll often find the clean**er** dirtier than the clean**ee**.

• **The dishrag.** Always full of crumbs and spills from those floor and counter wipes and rarely fully rinsed, never mind cleaned or replaced. There it sits, darkening and fermenting in the sink or dish drainer for weeks on end, awaiting a chance to contaminate the tabletop. We've all been offended by this in restaurants, without always taking a good look at what we've got on our own drainboard at home. To keep dishrags sweet-smelling and germ-free, you can wash them with the laundry load you bleach. If they're too far gone, throw them away!

• **Bowl brush/toilet plunger.** They have seen some pretty poopy action in the line of duty. But they're seldom adequately rinsed, never mind cleaned or put away. They just lean against the wall back there exposed to flies, kids, etc.

• **Scrub brushes:** Even if we do actually rinse them after we use them, they've got all kinds of odd little leftovers from cleaning operations nestled down amidst the roots of their bristles. Give them a scalp massage every so often with a sturdy steel comb and wash them in hot, sudsy water. Then give 'em a high-pressure rinse and set them bristle up to dry.

• **Sponges and pot scrubbers** can get almost as ripe as dishrags, though they can disguise it better, because all the sourness and debris is hidden away inside. Don't count on that occasional bath in the dishwater to keep your sponges and scrubbers clean. Squeeze some fresh, soapy water through them from time to time and soak them in baking soda solution if they get to smelling bad; you can even toss them in the clothes washer.

• **Mop heads** are often brown or beige before their time from failure to clean or rinse after floor cleaning or other heavy duty action. That halfhearted squeeze we give them won't remove all those clinging insect wings and mold spores. So slosh that mop head well in clean, soapy water, rinse it well in clear water, and wring it and spread it somewhere, preferably outside in the sun, to dry.

• **Dust mops** can get lint-filled enough to become dirt distributors, so shake, brush, or vacuum yours regularly to keep it gathering aggressively. You can also tuck the head inside a mesh laundry bag and run it through the washer with warm water and detergent but no bleach. Then let it air dry, and never use your **dust** mop to sop up spills!

• Even **brooms** especially the plastic split-tip kind, can profit from a comb out of the fuzz and debris that's accumulated at the business end from time to time.

• **The handles** of mops, brooms, dustpans, etc. always see a lot of action on the front lines of filth and are in constant contact with dirty hands. Ever clean yours?

• **Buckets:** Amazing how we assume that because a bucket gets filled with cleaning solution it never has to be cleaned. How many buckets have slimy or gritty "tub rings" or the grimy remains of the last batch of washwater still in them? The moisture that condenses on the bottom of a bucket, too, often glues stuff from Fig Newton crumbs to mouse manure to it. Now that bucket is sitting in all kinds of new places, spreading stains (including rust stains) and germs. Take a look before you turn on the faucet!

• **Dust cloths.** Yes, even these can and will spread more problems than they pick up. Ever wonder what's in dust? Lots of germs, tiny abrasive particles, and other bad stuff (not just innocent lint) are in there, and they can be spread to, or even scratch, other surfaces. Dust cloths should have a short life—that's why I recommend the disposable kind. If you use a fabric cloth, keep it good and clean and switch surfaces often.

• **Furniture polishing rags** are often ranker than a mechanic's rag and doused with several different kinds of polishing compounds over time, thus ensuring a streaked finish on the credenza. Keep your wax, oil, etc., rags all sacred and apart for that one single purpose and remember that polishing cloths, too, should be retired regularly. The cleanest rags give the brightest shine! Don't try to recycle hopelessly greasy, stiff, blackened, or threadbare rags—toss 'em out, in a metal container if they're oily or solvent laden, and replace them with fresh, clean ones.

• **The vacuum** often needs to have the beater-bar cleaned (see p. 33), and imagine how embarrassing a dusty cleaning machine must be as vacuums usually are. And what about the matted fur and fluff in those attachment brushes?

Check out your cleaning arsenal and make sure you're wiping dirt off, not wiping it on!

How should I clean my wood chopping/butcher block surfaces ? #64

Many of us have a wooden cutting board set right into our kitchen countertop or stashed in our kitchen cupboards somewhere, and we butcher more than meat on it—salads, crusts, carrots, and scraps all get worked on (and into) it. The value of a "butcher block" is the very fact that wood is hard enough to work on but soft enough to allow knives and sharp tools to be used on it and even to pierce it, without dulling the knife or chipping the block. Hence a block surface has only an oil treatment—none of the usual wood finishes like varnish or paint can be used on it. So the blows of our preparation instruments aren't the only thing it absorbs—food particles, fats, meat and vegetable juices, etc., can soak in and provide a fine encouragement for bacteria growth and odors. This is the very reason those romantic-looking inlaid wood blocks

147

are a thing of the past for professional meat cutters—the pores and cavities in wood provide too many hiding places for salmonella bacteria. Butchers now use plastic (nylon) cutting blocks exclusively because they're so much easier to disinfect. A block should always be disinfected after cutting raw meat on it to keep any bacteria left behind from infecting other foods. A plastic cutting board is the best choice for the home, too, because it can be put right in the sink with hot, soapy water. If you have a wooden block inset in your counter, you may want to use it for vegetables only or just consider it a decoration.

If you do use a wood block to cut on, here's how to care for it. Since most chopping blocks are made of hard, tight-grained wood, moisture and food residue can't penetrate *too* easily. So if you remove those little shreds and seeps right away and give the board a quick wetting and thorough wiping with a solution of plain old dishwashing detergent and water right after you use it, you'll be a long way toward keeping it clean. Don't let the solution or any liquid sit on there for long, or it'll soak in and swell and raise the grain of the wood—it can even split your brawny block right down the middle. So just wipe it down quickly, rinse, and dry immediately with a clean cloth or paper toweling.

Don't let your block's surface get too crisscrossed or you'll just be providing underground canals for germs and odors. Sand or scrape it back to a much more sanitary smoothness from time to time.

A 1:10 bleach/water solution spread on the surface and then rinsed away is a good way to disinfect a wooden block. And a little lemon juice can help dispose of any lingering odors.

To keep your block from getting brittle and help heal its aches and pains from being beat on, treat it like an athlete—give it a rubdown from time to time. Any vegetable oil can be used for this, but mineral oil is even better—it's not only nontoxic; it never goes rancid. You don't ever want to use linseed or tung oil on your board if you actually cut on it, and animal fats such as bacon grease or lard are out, too. Apply the oil generously with a soft cloth when the board is good and dry, rub in it with fine steel wool, and leave it on there at least half an hour. If your block has been a long time between oilings, you might want to repeat the process or leave the oil on overnight. Then blot away any excess and rub the block dry. This will condition your block and keep it "chop chop" for quite a while.

What do I need to know when I'm hiring professional help with the cleaning ❓ ○ *#65*

All that glitters isn't gold, nor is every proclaimed professional a real professional! Ninety percent of new cleaning businesses fail in the first five years, so you can't just call up the first place listed in the Yellow Pages and count on getting a pro. You do need to know a few things if you plan to go beyond your family circle for cleaning help.

First, the problem of picking the real pros from the herd notwithstanding, it is a wise idea to seek out **professional** help for the purpose. The only thing worse than a poor-quality professional is giving the job to a hard-up relative. An experienced pro can save you time, money, and wrenched muscles and maybe even heated family arguments and acci-

149

dents. We rarely make our own bread, sew our own clothes, cut our own hair, or churn our own butter anymore, so it's not unimaginable to shift the tough cleaning jobs to outside help, too. Exactly what help?

There are platoons of cleaning people around—the ads and listings in newspapers, bulletin boards, and phone books under house cleaning, carpet cleaning, window cleaning, etc., will amaze you. Who do you choose out of these hundreds of selections? Usually, you want a maid or maid service for daily or weekly light or keep-up cleaning—dusting, vacuuming, kitchen and bathroom cleaning, floors, etc. For once-in-a-while deep cleaning, such as wax stripping, wall washing, or windows, you look for a housecleaning contractor. There are also specialty firms that do nothing but carpet and upholstery, blinds, or on-location drapery cleaning. Once you know the kind of service you want there are four questions to ask:

• "How long have you been in business?" Less than two years in the present location would make me nervous.

• "Give me four references!"

• "Give me a bid!" So before anyone starts the job, everyone understands exactly what is to be done, when it's scheduled to start and finish, and how much it will cost.

• "Who will come on the job?" Is it the sharp-looking person who gives you the bid or some drifter or untrained teenager they hired yesterday?

Do take the time to check the references to assure yourself that the cleaning service is competent and reliable. This will probably be a long-term rather than one-time relationship, so an hour up front will be time well invested, just like taking the time to find the right hairdresser. To get the best price shop around. Ask several firms to give you bids. Don't let price be your only guide, though—go with someone you like and trust.

If it's maid work you're after, should you contract with one of the mushrooming maid services or seek out and hire an independent?

Advantages of a maid service:

• If one cleaner gets sick or quits, they send someone else—the work still gets done.

• They have the hassle of finding, hiring, and training (and retaining) maids.

• You don't have to worry about deducting social security and taxes, insurance coverage, etc., either.

• They bring their own cleaning equipment and supplies (and lunch).

• They'll be supervised by a trained leader or supervisor.

Disadvantages:

• You won't get the individualized personal attention your own maid might give.

• Maid services offer set services—and may simply refuse special or unusual requests.

• You probably won't get the same worker each time.

• Extra services, such as windows, laundry, oven cleaning, or dishes will probably mean extra charges.

An hourly rate is the best deal for a homemaker—you're getting what you pay for. Maid services like to work on a flat fee so they can work faster/cut corners and boost their profit on the job. And as for tipping, most residential maids only expect a tip if they do something extra or maybe at Christmas.

Whichever way you decide to go:

• Before you assign the job, ask for proof of insurance. Bonding is a plus, too. If the workers are fully bonded and insured, any proven damage or theft should be covered.

• *Never, never, never* pay in advance.

• A written and signed contract is a good idea, too. Most professional services have a proposal form that lists the tasks to be performed and price of each. It becomes a binding agreement when you sign the acceptance portion.

To get the most out of a maid service, remember to do your part—pick up and put stray belongings away before they arrive so they can get right into their work. Don't expect them to do your dejunking and know where things go. And see that any personal or confidential stuff and all money and valuables are tucked away out of sight.

Get a cleaner you trust and leave him alone—do any of us work well with someone breathing down our neck? If you don't like something they've done, tell them what you're unhappy with and why and ask them to redo it. It usually only takes once.

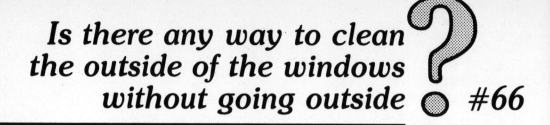

First off, forget the little magnetic gadgets you see advertised that supposedly do a miracle job on the outside glass while you run a cleaning pad over the inside. They're probably better than no cleaning at all for those panes you just can't reach any other way, but they don't do a good enough job to use for serious glass cleaning. If they did, you can bet the pros would be using them, instead of dangling over the edge of high buildings on cables and swing scaffolds.

Actually, quite a few different types of windows can be cleaned from the inside if you just use a little ingenuity. Most casement windows can be opened wide enough so you can slip your arm out between the window and the casing to wash the outside. If the crack is too narrow or your arm is too wide, get one of your skinny kids to do it or try using a twelve-inch extension handle on your squeegee and window-washing wand.

Our old familiar double-hung windows can be cleaned from the inside, too, if you slide the sashes back and forth to alternately expose all portions of the upper and lower sliders. But both sashes have to operate to do this, so if your upper ones are painted shut, you'll have to pry them loose first. Inside or outside, you can cut them loose with a wide putty knife carefully placed and gently tapped all along the problem area. If the frame is good and sound, a block of wood laid on the bottom edge of the jammed sash and, again, tapped gently should do it. Once they're sliding free, you're in business. If the screens have outside fasteners, convert them to the hook-and-eye type that you can unlatch from the inside. It's better security, anyway. Some people sit on the window sill to clean the outside of double-hungs, but don't do that without making sure you're secured by a stout rope and a safety belt to a sturdy anchor inside in case you slip. It's much safer to keep your feet firmly on the floor and just lean slightly out of the window, if you can reach it all that way.

Modern horizontal sliding windows are designed for easy cleaning from inside. You simply remove the sliding sash, usually by lifting it up and out of the track, and lean it against an inside wall for cleaning. If a screen is in place, it has to be removed before the sliding window will come out. The outside of the fixed sash can be cleaned with a window-washing wand and a squeegee by simply reaching out through the opening. For large windows you might have to use a short extension pole to reach the whole outside. If the screens and sash are hard to remove, make the job easier next time by lubricating them with silicone spray lubricant.

For windows it's impossible to get from the inside do what the pros do—invest twenty-five dollars in a long extension pole to fit your squeegee and washing wand. With one of these you can wash all your high windows without a ladder, without ever leaving solid ground. And to outwit any shrubbery, window wells, or stairwells that might be in your way, get the Super System handles for your squeegee and window washer. These allow you to adjust your tool so you can clean from any angle, reach right over or around obstructions, and squeegee even the oddest shape window with ease. A four-to-eight-foot pole will handle windows up to fifteen feet high, and one of the longer three-section handles will reach almost any second-story window.

Any higher than that, I'd pray for an angel or hire a pro.

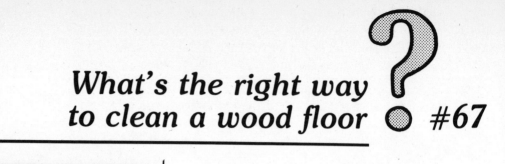

What's the right way to clean a wood floor ? #67

A way that gets the dirt off without hurting it—and just what that might be has caused some hot debates, because it depends on the kind of finish used on the wood. In the past especially, a penetrating oil was usually applied to wood floors to seal the surface and then a paste (solvent or "spirit") wax over it for a little extra shine and protection. The oil and paste wax approach is a time-honored tradition, and most

154

manufacturers of wood flooring still recommend this "no-water" system of wood floor care. Why? Because any cleaners or waxes containing water can swell, warp, discolor, and raise the grain of unsealed wood. Many of us today, however, are choosing to seal our wood floors with polyurethane, a tough, varnishlike finish which needs no waxing and can be cleaned with water.

I don't think there's any question that a floor finished with urethane is easier to care for than one maintained with paste wax. Two or three good coats of urethane on your floor form a strong, waterproof finish that holds a nice gloss without waxing, withstands traffic well, and can be damp-mopped just like any other no-wax floor.

But this is only true of floors that had the urethane applied *after they were installed.* Many wood floors are laid with prefinished, factory-finished, planks or tiles—you can usually tell because the cracks between the boards are beveled or v-grooved. The finish used on the wood may be perfectly water-safe, but if the cracks between the boards have never been sealed, water running down between the boards could penetrate and buckle the unsealed wood underneath. You have to use water very sparingly on a floor of this type until it's finally been refinished and the cracks sealed.

Even if the floor was finished in place, go easy on the water—the finish on any wood floor develops tiny cracks over time from the inevitable swelling and shrinking of the boards with the daily changes in temperature and humidity. So slopping water indiscriminately on the floor can cause it to seep down into the cracks and damage the wood. A floor with a sound coating of urethane can be spot cleaned and damp mopped with water, as long as you exercise reasonable care. Just get the water on and off quickly, don't leave drips or puddles standing on the floor, and use a mild neutral cleaner such as a capful of liquid dishwashing detergent in a bucket of warm water. The only care a urethane-finished floor should need other than that is a thorough cleaning and recoating with urethane once every several years.

If your wood floor has been finished with penetrating oil and paste wax, your best bet is to keep on waxing it. And use a paste wax, period. Paste waxing is hard work, but not nearly as hard as trying to get all of the wax off so a urethane coating will bond properly to the floor. I'd only consider refinishing a waxed floor with urethane if it's in such bad shape that it needs an overall sanding, and then I'd probably hand the job over to a pro.

A waxed floor in good condition only needs a weekly buffing and then rewaxing two or three times a year. Paste wax is harder to apply than liquid spirit wax, but it gives a much longer-lasting shine. "One-step" cleaner/polisher products are easiest of all to use, but also wear off the fastest. If you're going to go to all the trouble of moving the furniture out and getting the room ready, you might as well do it right and have it

155

last awhile. And no matter what the label says, never use water-base floor finishes on a wood floor—the resulting buildup and eventual wet-stripping required won't be worth whatever results you get in the meantime.

You can use one of the light grasshopperlike home polishing machines for buffing if you can bear it, but when you get ready to rewax, go to the rental store and get a heavy-duty commercial thirteen- to seventeen-inch single-disc floor polisher. It'll make an otherwise brutal job bearable.

First put a dry steel wool pad on the buffer and clean the floor; use wood floor cleaner under the pad only if the old wax is heavily soiled and discolored. Then vacuum up any debris, spread a small amount of wax on a fresh steel wool pad, and clean and wax a small area of the floor at a time with the machine, spreading the wax in a circular pattern until no swirls or spatters can be seen. Let the wax dry for the time recommended on the label and then buff with a white polishing pad or a buffing brush.

For routine maintenance, regular vacuuming or dust mopping is a must. Dust and grit ground in underfoot is the #1 enemy of wood floors—it scratches and abrades the finish and wears off and sullies the wax. This is true of all floors, but especially paste-waxed wood—keeping dirt off is the most important thing you can do. Good entrance mats and maybe a few area rugs, too, will help keep damaging soil away from your hard-won shine. On wood you don't want rubber or foam-backed rugs or mats, however—they can cloud the finish on a wood floor. And though you never want to damp mop a paste-waxed floor, if you wipe up spills immediately with a damp cloth you can keep most spills from becoming spots.

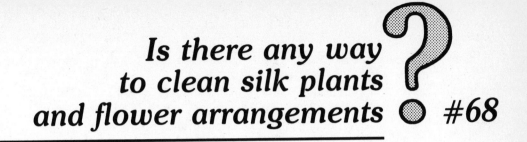

Is there any way to clean silk plants and flower arrangements ❓ ⬤ *#68*

We knew these were somehow too good to be true, and the catch indeed comes when it's time to clean them. Every home and building has some of these now, and they're a lot like a crystal chandelier—lovely to look at, but almost impossible to clean. All those little folds and frills and buds and blossoms and bracts and tendrils collect dust like mad, and they get their share, too, of that airborne oily film that only makes them better dust catchers. The first few layers of dust may only add to their lifelike quality; then they begin to look ugly.

So what do we do when we're tired of averting our eyes every time we amble past them? It's hard to know what fabric flowers can take in the way of cleaning without knowing what they're made of.

So the next time you buy one of these arrangements, read the tag, if there is one, before you toss it or come right out and ask what the flowers are made of and how to clean them. Your friendly local flower shop owner might actually know, even if the holiday fill-in at the department store doesn't. Unless the store made a big point of saying they were silk, they're probably some kind of synthetic, such as polyester. That may not sound as classy, but it's a big help when it comes time to clean them. Synthetics hold their shape and color far better than silk, which will never quite look the same after many cleaning operations.

In general, how you go about it and how far you go will have a lot to do with the nature of the bouquet, how expensive it was, how patient you are, and how well your nervous system would survive the possibility that those crocuses may never adorn your coffee table again. Fabric flower cleaning is usually best done when you're feeling reflective or nostalgic or there's some big important job you're trying to postpone.

Dust. If there isn't an oily film on it, simple dusting can do a lot to restore an arrangement to decorative. For this you can use an electrostatic dust cloth (see p. 56), a feather duster, a small artist's sable brush, a hair dryer set on cool and low, or even a can of the compressed air they use to dust computers. Whichever you use, check for fallen flower heads or dropped buds when you finish. Stick them back on now, or they'll end up inside the vacuum or kicking around the house forever before you finally throw them away.

On the other hand, if the gladioli have been gathering grunge for longer than you care to remember, you might want to **wash** them. You won't want to do this if they actually are silk, since they'll almost surely lose some of their shape or luster along the way. But if they seem to be sturdily constructed, you could try hand-wiping your flowers in place as follows.

Hand-wipe. Dip a small cloth, such as a piece of clean terrycloth, into a bowl of Woolite and cool water and wring it out as hard as you can. Then wipe your way around the bouquet—a wonderful way to finally get acquainted with what's actually in there. Support with one hand while you wipe with the other and reshape each daisy or whatever, if necessary, before you move on to the next. Go easy on the edges unless you like your leaves and petals frayed. If you can marshal the strength of character, work your way into the bouquet at least a little beyond the surface, and remember that flowerheads may be more fun and flashier, but if you don't get the leaves, too, it's not going to all look like new again. Be especially careful with flower centers, stamens, tendrils, and berries—any of which may be extra-perilously attached or less amenable to being wetted.

If you come across a bunch of prickly pods or a patch of Spanish moss, skip right over it and don't look back.

Dip wash (for individual flowers or bouquets you dare to disassemble) Fill a sink with a solution of Woolite and cool water and dip each flower into it, stem and all. Swish it around a few times gently, then dip it into a sink or pan of cool rinse water. (Some people like to add a

158

teaspoon of white vinegar per quart to the rinse water.) Then shake well and hang by the stem to dry.

Spray. Should you spray-clean your fabric flowers with a fine mist of soap and water from a spray bottle or the aerosol cleaners that you just "spray on and let dry"? With either of these procedures, the dirt isn't being removed; it's just soaking into the surface. The begonias may look better for a while, but sooner or later it'll catch up with you. And as for the protective sprays suggested for fabric flowers, from hairspray to products specially concocted for the purpose, these may keep stains away and the dust from settling all the way in, but the flowers will still get dusty. And some of these sprays can alter the color and texture of your flowers.

Prevent. You can swear off fabric flowers or put dust-attracting decorations like these under glass or plastic and keep them out of rooms with wood or oil stoves.

Is upholstered furniture cleaning best left to the pros, or can I do it myself? #69

Upholstered furniture has two main enemies—oil and dust. The oil—skin oil, hair oil, makeup, even oil from lounging pets—builds up on the armrests, headrest, and seat cushions during normal use. And those persistent little particles of dust accumulate just as rapidly on upholstered pieces as they do on the black lacquered coffee table—they're just snuggled down into those plush surfaces so you don't notice them. If you doubt this, just drag your favorite armchair into a beam of sunlight and slap the seat cushion smartly with your hand. You can create your own little dust storm in a second. All this dust and oil combines to form a greasy glaze that coats the fibers of upholstered furniture in the three "trouble zones"—headrest, armrest, and seat—and is mighty hard to remove if you let it build up long.

So the first thing you want to do is remove dust from the fabric with your vacuum cleaner before it can get together with the oily soils and get set in its ways. A canister vac with an upholstery head is best for getting corners and crevices, but you can't beat a beater bar for removing deep-down dust in the cushions. One of the hand-held cordless vacs with a beater bar or even your upright raised to the occasion will really knock out imbedded dirt. Don't use a beater bar vac on delicate or loosely woven fabrics, though, or anything with long loose threads or tassels that could get wound around the beater. If you vacuum your furniture every week or so, dust won't have a chance to accumulate.

When soiled areas begin to appear in the danger zones, a little spot cleaning is in order. Before spotting, though, vacuum the area thoroughly—remember that cloud of dust? If you wet the fabric without removing it, it'll all turn to mud right on there. Then look at the care label to see what type of cleaning is recommended. If the label is coded, here's what the symbols mean: W—clean with water-based cleaners (shampoo); S—clean with dry-cleaning solvent **only**; WS—either method is o.k.; X—no liquids, vacuuming or light brushing **only**. If the piece says dry clean only, you'll have to confine your touchup to dry cleaning solvent. If it's shampooable, which 75 percent of upholstery fabrics are, you can use upholstery shampoo, either a concentrate you mix with water or a ready-to-use aerosol foam. If there's no label, shampoo in an inconspicuous area and let it dry to see if wet cleaning will cause shrinking, water rings, fabric distortion, or color change. If not, feel free to shampoo. It's always wise to test an untried upholstery cleaner before using it overall to make sure it won't do any damage.

To spot clean, moisten a terry towel with dry cleaning solvent and scrub the soiled area lightly—you want to rub the dirt off, not rub it in. Then be sure to feather out the edges of the spot you've cleaned so it doesn't stand out from the surrounding fabric. For shampooable fabrics, follow the dry spotter with a sponging with upholstery shampoo, then rinse with a towel dampened in clear water. If you mix shampoo from a concentrate, wring your cleaning sponge out in the solution several times to create a foam and apply only the foam to the fabric, not the water itself. It's important not to overwet the fabric, as too much water can cause stains to bleed out of the stuffing material. Durable fabrics can be shampooed with a soft brush if more ambitious scrubbing is required. With some fabrics, you may have to thoroughly clean the soiled area, then lightly shampoo and rinse the entire panel you're working on—arm, seat cushion, back, etc.—to avoid leaving a water ring. Dry with a clean towel and, if it's a napped fabric, brush the pile all in one direction so it stands up evenly. If you have a wet/dry vac, it'll do a better job of removing excess shampoo and drying the fabric than a towel will.

If your cushions have removable covers, resist the urge to take them off and throw them in the washer. It's better to shampoo them on the cushion and let them dry to shape to avoid shrinking the fabric.

If you give your upholstered pieces a little cat bath like this as soon as they start to show dirty spots, you can avoid deep cleaning for a long time. Keeping the seat, arms, and backrest of an upholstered item spot cleaned is 90 percent of the battle, because the sides and back hardly ever get dirty—they just need regular vacuuming.

When the time comes for a thorough deep cleaning, it's probably best to call in a pro furniture cleaner, especially if it's a dry clean only piece. If a piece is so dirty that it needs extraction cleaning or is covered with a delicate or expensive fabric, that's a job better left to a trained professional, too. But if the recliner in the family room needs a going over and you want to do it yourself, there's no reason not to as long as it's shampooable and the fabric is a fairly durable one. If it's not too badly soiled, you can go over an entire chair or couch carefully yourself, using the spot cleaning techniques described above.

After deep cleaning furniture, it's always a good idea to reapply Scotchgard or a similar soil retardant, to keep future hand, head, and hind quarter headaches to a minimum.

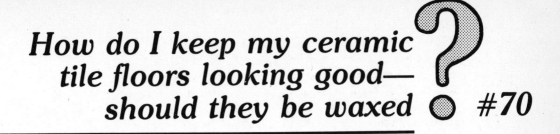

How do I keep my ceramic tile floors looking good— should they be waxed ? #70

The tiles on the space shuttles get all the media attention, but questions about bathroom tile put a lot more people in orbit. If you added in concerns about tile in our kitchens, entryways, utility rooms, and halls, you'd be spaced out for sure. The overall toughness and permanence of tile makes it a mighty efficient and energy-saving surface, especially for floors. If you've got it, you've got a good thing, so don't throw up your hands over a few frustrating experiences.

Ceramic tile needs no waxing, requires very little daily maintenance,

163

and would be close to a perfect floor if not for that pesky mortar used to fill the joints between the tile.

Glazed tile has a glasslike coating bonded to the surface during firing, and it can have a high gloss or a soft matte finish, be either slick and smooth or subtly textured. Matte-finish glazed ceramic is the best floor tile for a home. You don't want high-gloss glazed tile on a floor, because it'll eventually scratch and dull in the traffic areas and look bad. And as for color, light to medium earth tones show dirt and wear least; stark white or extremely dark colors will mean extra effort to keep them looking good. Larger tiles are better—the more tile the less grout! A ceramic tile floor will be underfoot a long time, so make sure you get a good tile and install it right. Cheap tiles with button backing or a poor glaze will crack and wear and leave you unhappy before long. A flat— flat-back, rather than button-back—tile with a good thick glaze is a forever floor and about as care-free as you can get. All you need to do is sweep or vacuum regularly to remove dirt and grit and damp-mop it every so often with a mild detergent.

As for that grout, even though it's the weak point in the system, there are things you can do to help. When installing a new floor, always ask for grout with a latex or acrylic admix, which makes it denser and more stain-resistant. And be sure to color the grout to match the tile. White grout won't stay white long—it shows every little smudge and mildew speck. After a floor has been down for a few weeks and is cured, apply a silicone masonry waterproofer to the grout. This will seal it so that water and stains can't penetrate as easily. If you have discolored grout now, give it a thorough scrubbing with a stiff brush and heavy-duty cleaner, followed by the silicone seal as soon as it dries.

Because of the grout, again, you always have to be a little careful when you're choosing cleaners. The tile itself is impervious to just about any common cleaning chemical, but the cement in grout can be damaged much more easily. So don't use strong alkaline cleaners like TSP or washing soda or strong acids such as muriatic or hydrochloric. The installer may use a muriatic acid "brick and tile cleaner" to remove any stray spatters of grouting when he finishes up his job, but that's the last time it should be used. You shouldn't need to use any kind of harsh cleaner on your ceramic floor tile anyway, aside from a once-in-a-while scrubbing with heavy-duty cleaner and a brush to remove any obstinate soil in the joints. You can also scrub with a nylon brush or nylon scrub pad, but never steel wool or powdered cleanser. And here an oil-treated dust mop or oily sweeping compound will only discolor the grout and attract dust.

Grout gripes aside, 90 percent of tile unhappiness otherwise is residue streaks from cleaning. So for regular mopping just use a little bit of neutral detergent—liquid dishwashing detergent will do fine—and keep the mop water clean so it doesn't leave a dulling film. Don't use

164

soaps—soap flakes, Ivory Liquid, etc—because soaps leave a cloudy dirt-collecting layer. If your floor still looks hazy after mopping, either buffing with a floor polisher or giving it a mop-rinse with a bucket of clear water to which one cup of vinegar has been added should restore the luster. Just do remember that matte-finish tile absorbs light and is going to look matte, not shiny, even if perfectly cleaned and rinsed.

Glazed ceramic tiles don't need any sealer or finish, and it's usually impossible to get any kind of floor finish to stick to their smooth, impervious surface anyway. Most coatings will wear off quickly and look ugly, so if you have matte-finished glazed tile far better to learn to love it than to lust after the glossy look. Some unglazed tiles will hold sealer and finish, but this just starts a process of repeated recoating and eventual stripping of the finish, which you don't need. If you can learn to appreciate the soft glow of unglazed tile, you'll find it much easier to maintain as is.

How do I get rid of mildew *#71*

You've heard of being able to hear corn growing in Kansas on a hot day? Call me crazy, but I swear that as I sat in a quiet little wood church on the island of Lanai in Hawaii not long ago I heard a strange noise on the wall next to me. When I went over and pulled the bottom of the curtain back there was a prime patch of mildew growing, and yes, folks, I could actually hear those little spores multiplying and yeasting their way to a black, velvety fungus-flocked wall covering, right there in the sanctuary.

You may not have it this bad, but mildew isn't dirt; it is indeed a fungus growth that thrives wherever there's lots of moisture and not much light or ventilation and temperatures of seventy-five to eighty-five degrees. And if all growth conditions are right, it's like wild morning glory in the garden—it crops up everywhere and comes back again and again. It isn't that awful musty odor or even the black, blue, brown, or orange speckles over everything that makes mildew so menacing. The word *fungus* means this is a little **plant** you're looking at, and it puts tiny roots down into whatever it's growing on. Those roots feed on—digest, destroy, remove—the cellulose and protein in paper, leather fabric, wood, etc. The longer mildew is on something, the greater the chance that it'll be weakened, rotted, deteriorated, or reduced to a skeleton of its former self. Mildew can eat all of the strength out of jute carpet backing, for instance, in as little as two weeks.

A lot of us, too, are allergic to the mildew snuggled into our rugs, books, beds, tile, and even upholstered furniture.

A wipedown of all mildew-prone surfaces with disinfectant during your weekly cleaning will do a lot to keep mildew at bay, but the only sure cure for mildew is to eliminate the conditions that encourage it. This means:

1. Reduce dampness. Ventilate bathrooms, basements, crawl spaces, closets, etc., with vents, exhaust fans, louvered doors, dehumidifiers—even opening the windows helps, as long as it's less than 110 percent humidity outside. Installing a heat cable or a low-wattage bulb that can be left burning in a closet or storage area reduces dampness, too. Seal any concrete floor you intend to carpet over in a mildew-prone location. And keep an eye out for moisture seeping indoors through roof leaks, poorly placed downspouts, improperly functioning gutters, etc.

2. Let it shine. Sunlight kills mildew, and even indirect outside light or bright artificial light will help discourage its growth inside. If you have a mildew problem, you don't want heavy curtains or awnings over the windows and shades half down all day. Overgrown trees, shrubs, and trellises right up against the house won't help a bit either.

3. Let it dry. Never throw clothes in the hamper wet, or leave the shower curtain bunched up after showering; never put tents, sleeping bags, raincoats, umbrellas, boots, shoes, etc., away wet. Hang damp things up or set them out, in the sun, if possible, and give them a chance to get completely dry before you put them away.

4. Choose inhospitable materials. Mildew won't grow on most synthetics, so for a basement or the like you want carpeting, backing, and padding all made entirely of man-made fibers such as nylon, polypropylene, and urethane. When painting or papering mildew-prone spots, use mildew resistant paints and adhesives.

When you get a mildew attack, here's how to handle it:

1. On showers, siding, painted walls, and other hard surfaces apply a disinfectant cleaner or a solution of a half to one cup of chlorine bleach to each quart of water. Then scrub with a stiff brush and rinse well. Make sure you have some ventilation while you're doing this, and never leave bleach solution on plastic or chrome long. This will kill the mildew, and the bleach will lighten any stains, but it won't keep mildew from growing there again.

2. Clothing and shower curtains. Brush off all you can and air out in the sun. Launder washables with regular laundry detergent plus a half a cup of bleach, if colorfast. Dry clean nonwashables. Launder plastic shower curtains as you normally would, but be sure to use some bleach as well as detergent.

3. Shoes, handbags, etc. Wipe down with a 50/50 solution of isopropyl alcohol and water. Wipe with a clean, damp cloth and buff dry.

4. Upholstery, mattresses, etc. Air out in bright sunlight. Vacuum thoroughly with disposable vacuum bag to remove spores and throw bag away. Wipe any areas of active growth with dry cleaning solvent (or an alcohol/water solution, if the fabric will withstand wet cleaning).

P.S. Some of that black stuff that crops up on the bathroom caulking isn't mildew, by the way. Much of that tub and tile caulk you buy, even the expensive stuff, will turn black about eighteen months from the day of installation, no matter what you do. It's a chemical change that happens with time. So next time make sure you get yourself some **silicone** sealer—it won't go dark.

How do I get smoke odor out of my rooms and furnishings ? #72

Any smoke inside the house is a special problem, because smoke is full of tiny particles of carbon, ash, resins, oils, tar, and nicotine. These oily particles are carried everywhere by the air currents and deposit themselves on surfaces all over. And they drift into every nook and cranny, wherein they lie, unreachable, emitting noxious fumes for weeks, months, or even years. Smoke stains and odors from cigarettes, a stove or fireplace, or a minor cooking conflagration can invade the entire house and be difficult indeed to get rid of.

If you have a smoke or soot problem of any size, such as from a furnace blowup, your best bet is to let a professional smoke damage contractor handle it. Most such mishaps are covered by homeowner's insurance, and a professional smoke and fire restoration contractor has the specialized equipment and expertise needed to handle severe smoke damage. You can handle less serious soot, cigarette, or fireplace smoke odors yourself with the right tools and a little know-how.

First, air out the entire home and remove as much of the surface residue as you can. It's especially important to thoroughly vacuum upholstered furniture, drapes, and carpeting, because such soft, porous materials will be saturated with odor-causing smoke particles, **even though you can't see them.** This is why you never want to sit on smoked upholstery before it's been cleaned, or you just grind the stuff into the fabric. Vacuuming is better than dusting, even on hard surfaces, because it's better at getting the smoke particles out of all the little pores and crevices. Large ceiling and wall areas can be brushed or dry-sponged to remove the smoke film (see p. 219). As soon as one part of the sponge gets black and reaches its saturation point, fold over to a fresh section of the sponge and keep on going.

After removing as much of the loose soot as possible, clean all washable surfaces with a warm solution of all-purpose cleaner, to which you've added a water-soluble deodorizer such as *Big D* or *Nilium* or one of the specialized smoke odor removers. Products like these actually neutralize the odor; they don't just try to mask it with another fragrance like the run-of-the-mill aerosol room deodorizers. These professional formulations, which you can find at a janitorial-supply store, attack the odor-causing material at a molecular level, altering it into a form that has no unpleasant odor. This treatment will usually be all that's needed to completely clean and deodorize hard surfaces. For porous hard surfaces such as stone, brick, and unfinished wood, a spray-on smoke odor counteractant—also from the janitorial-supply store—can be applied after cleaning.

On things like windows, light fixtures, and blinds the yellow staining caused by cigarette smoke is often more of a problem than the odor. An alcohol-based window cleaner like Windex or one you buy in bulk at, yes, the janitorial-supply store is especially good at dissolving tar and nicotine buildups. If you add an extra bit of isopropyl rubbing alcohol it'll cut the smoke film even better.

The real odor removal riddle is the soft stuff—upholstery, carpeting, and drapes. Fabrics and filling materials—especially foam rubber upholstery and carpet padding—trap and hold smoke odors with alarming efficiency. To neutralize the odor-causing particles here, you have to get the deodorizing agent deep indeed, and this isn't easy. The most commonly used method is fogging, which is just what it sounds like—applying a deodorizer in a mist that floats around and envelopes everything, just as the smoke did. A janitorial-supply store should have smoke odor eliminators designed for fog application, too, and many of them also have fogging equipment for sale or rent. For what seems like a hopelessly entrenched smoke odor problem, though, it's again wise to call in a professional. He or she will have the hot foggers, solvent-based deodorizers, ozone generators, and other specialized equipment often needed to do a thorough job on heavy smoke saturations.

After you've cleaned and deodorized, it's a good idea to put a few "stick up" (gel) room deodorizers around to deal with any lingering odors. Set one under the refrigerator where the circulating air comes out and two in the air handler or ductwork of your furnace. Don't forget to change that smoked up furnace filter, too. To keep cigarette smoke from building up in the first place, an electrostatic air filter or small ion generator near the source of the smoke can be a great help.

What's the best thing to clean and shine Formica and other plastic laminates ? ● #73

What a liberating invention plastic laminate is; we ought to put a statue in the park of the person who thought up this labor saving surface. If the birds bombed our Formica memorial, we could clean it off a lot easier than those green-stained copper and bronze beauties. Almost any ordinary household cleaner will float the dirt off plastic laminate countertops, tabletops, and walls because it's so slick, smooth, and nonporous that not much sticks to it. That's the whole secret of their success—plastic laminates have such a dense or tight surface that cleaning operations are relatively simple.

The only problem is that when we do get a little stain or deposit on there—a drop of grape juice or blob of dried pancake batter—we lose our heads and attack it with steel wool or powdered cleanser. That's the one thing our lovely laminate doesn't need—its smooth, shiny finish sanded away with abrasives. Once it's roughed up and dull, soils and stains penetrate easily and will be tough to remove. Soaking is the big secret of cleaning this marvelous material. Apply a solution of plain old dish soap or all-purpose cleaner and water and let it sit awhile; it'll lift off those stuck-on foods and coffee stains so you'll never have to do much scrubbing.

And when you do have to scrub, the right way to do so is with a white—never green—nylon-backed scrub sponge. If you keep the laminate good and wet while you're rubbing with this, even mirror-finish Formica is very unlikely to ever be damaged. For a slatelike or other highly textured finish you might use a soft-bristled brush and leave the solution on a little longer. After the laminate is good and clean—and dry—you can apply appliance wax or furniture polish such as Pledge or Jubilee to seal out stains and protect the finish.

If you do get a spot on your laminate, give it a chance to go away by itself before you launch into possibly damaging stain removal maneuvers. It may take several days, but many stains will eventually lighten and disappear with repeated everyday cleanings. For stubborn stains like Kool-Aid red and USDA prime-beef purple, smear with a paste of baking soda and water or lemon juice and let it dry on there before you remove it. If that doesn't do it, try a paste of bleaching cleanser such as Ajax or Comet or automatic dishwasher detergent applied the same way. Diluted chlorine bleach can be used in extreme cases, but don't leave it on more than a minute.

To keep your laminate looking good, keep these things away from it: knives (cut on a cutting board), hot pans (use a trivet or hot pad underneath), cigarettes (no burning butts on the edge of the counter), tin cans and metal containers (you can't even trust a damp can of cleaner not to leave a rust stain), strong solvents (fingernail polish remover, lacquer thinner), strong alkalis or acids (such as oven, drain, or toilet bowl cleaner or rust remover), and abrasives of any kind.

But given half a chance and a little care, plastic laminate is long-lasting, durable, and genuinely maintenance-freeing material.

Is a cloth or paper towel better for drying 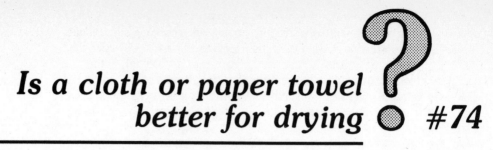 #74

Any pro will tell you cloth beats paper fifty to one in most cleaning cases. I like paper towels in two situations: 1) Quick on-the-spot wipes—when you don't have time to hunt for a cloth or take care of it after you use it, a disposable paper towel does fine and is easy to keep handy. You just grab it and use it and throw it away. 2) "One way" cleaning or simple removal, like wiping gobs of grease off a fan or the awful blackened oven cleaner out of the oven. Messes like these won't usually wash completely out of a cloth anyway, so disposing of the mess

174

with the paper towel is the answer. And if you're disposing of the dead spider under the TV or removing something unmentionable or unsanitary from the scene, if you use a paper towel you don't have to deal with it again.

Paper towel is a great short-range single-use product, but when you start your serious cleaning, cloth is far superior. Even the thinnest cloth can absorb more, faster, than a sheet of paper, and cloth doesn't disintegrate or leave little bits behind when the going gets tough on rough or textured surfaces. It gives your hands more protection, too, should you run across a protruding nailhead or sharp splinter in the course of your cleaning. Cloth is softer than paper—paper is made from **wood** fiber, remember?—so it's safer to use on Plexiglas and other delicate/sensitive surfaces. Cloth is cheaper than paper. Think of how many $1.34 a roll towels it takes to mop up a sizable spill. Cloth is environmentally sounder, too: It takes most of a good-sized tree to make a case of paper towel—the tree is gone forever and the used towels become a disposal problem. The cotton plants that would grow in a good-sized sandbox will make a dozen reusable terry towels, and they'll be back next year.

So you want cloth, but rayon, nylon, polyester, silk, linen, and the like are about worthless for wiping, since absorbency is what you're after. Materials like these were designed to shed moisture, not pick it up. The ultimate goal of cleaning is to dry the surface—and as quickly as possible. If you leave it wet, even clean, you'll end up with a dull, uneven, streaky finish. Cotton makes the best cleaning cloths of all because it's so soft and absorbent. Thick cotton terry toweling with all its thirsty little loops works wonders on things like dry-buffing and wall washing. Cotton diapers, cotton flannel, or cotton knits—alias old T-shirts—make the best polishing and dusting cloths. Cotton diapers or old lint-free linen napkins really shine on glass, mirrors, and chrome. Don't waste your time with cotton/poly blends—only 100 percent cotton fabrics are absorbent enough to really work well. Hotels, motels and linen services will often offer used towels, bathmats, napkins, and diapers for sale at a fraction of their cost new. Find some bargain terrycloth or use your old bath towels.

There's a secret to the size of a cleaning cloth, too—if they're too little they won't be able to handle even an average task, too big and it's like wearing an extra-long tie; they get in or sop up or knock over everything you don't want them to.

You can make yourself an unbeatable all-purpose cleaning cloth from an eighteen-by-eighteen-inch square of cotton terry toweling. Hem all the edges, then fold it over once. Then sew the long side together securely and you'll have a double thick, easy to handle nine-inch-by-eighteen-inch tube of terrycloth. It can be folded once or twice to fit the task and your hand, reversed and turned inside out for up to sixteen different surfaces! (see illustration) You can toss it into the washing machine and dryer when you're done and use it again and again. The only cloths I generally chuck after a single use are metal polish or paint or vanish cloths.

To make a cleaning cloth, cut an eighteen-by-eighteen-inch square of terrycloth and hem it on all sides. Then fold it over once and stitch it together securely down the long side. Fold the finished "tube" of terry over once, and then again, so it just fits your hand.

P.S. When you do need a paper towel, which of that endless aisle is best? You want a good and absorbent double-ply, nonpatterned one. Patterned towels can bleed color onto light surfaces. Only experience will tell you if it's absorbent, but Bounty, Viva, and Brawny are among the more reliable rolls to toss in your cart.

How do I get my hands and fingernails clean after a big, dirty cleanup job **?** ○ #75

... without removing all my skin in the process?

The cleanest-handed person I know is always up to his elbows in grease, paint, and garden mulch, yet he never has any potting soil clinging to his pinkies. Before he starts a project, he squirts a little liquid hand soap in his hand and rubs it until it dries like hand lotion. When he's finished, awful crud of all kinds comes right off and there's no deposits deep in the cracks and pores because the soft soap was there first and sealed off the opportunity!

Putting something on your skin "before" makes it a lot harder for dirt and stains to penetrate and is one of the better ways to avoid a half-hour at the sink and ugly irritated hands after. Some people use hand dishwashing detergent instead of liquid hand soap, but you may find it too drying. If it's simple garden dirt you're guarding against, you can just scratch your nails across a moist bar of soap before you head out for the muck beds. And since the world would never be without a product designed just for the purpose, you can also use Elmer's Invisible Glove, a clear nonslippery coating that you just wash off with soap and water when you're done. Even a good thick coat of Vaseline or lanolin cream applied ahead will do a lot to deflect dirt, since dry, rough skin and nails stain more easily.

The original and still hard to beat barrier is rubber gloves, of course, if only someone besides surgeons and burglars could bring themselves to use them. They are hot in summer and a little awkward for some chores, and I'll be the first to admit they cut us off from some of that very sensual but also useful contact with things. But you shouldn't do **really** dirty jobs without them, such as handling dangerous chemicals like oven cleaner or solvents, or applying wood stain, where the dye penetrates every pore and cuticle and will still be there six days later. The gloves with a flannel lining are a little heavier and more expensive, but many people find them more bearable to wear because they don't have that rubbery feeling.

When you choose your tools, too, why not reach for ones that at least minimize your personal immersion in harsh chemicals and filthy messes? Such as a utility brush with a nice sturdy handle, instead of a deck brush, or an extension handle for your paint roller. But what if you didn't prevent, so now you have a real mess on your hands?

• Stay away from solvents if at all possible. They not only dry and crack your skin; they're powerful poisons that can be absorbed right through it, as well as inhaled. Use solvents—sparingly—as a last resort and try to confine yourself to the less deadly ones, such as kerosene and paint thinner.

• Abrasive bar soaps or powders will often get it off—but they're no easier on your hands than they are on your household surfaces, and this is live skin we're dealing with here.

• Give good old soap and water a chance at it before you move to anything more violent. If it's grease you're dealing with, a detergent such as liquid dish detergent will do better than soap per se.

• Use your hands and fingers to scrub each other as much as possible, rather than a stiff, scratchy brush. And a neutral pH soap such as Dove or Caress will be easier on your skin than just any old soap that happens to be around, which will usually be fairly alkaline. Our skin is naturally mildly acid, and it helps to keep germs away if it stays that way.

• A couple of well-aimed blasts of WD40 will make quick work of grease, paint, and tar removal. Handymen swear by it.

• If something stronger still seems called for, consider the waterless cleaners used by car mechanics and others for whom greasy, grimy hands are an everyday event. These go by gutsy names like Go Jo, Top Grit, and Goop, and they're thick pastes that you massage in and wipe off before you ever do any washing. The cleaning action usually comes from a solvent or abrasive granules of some kind, and most include a skin conditioner, too. There are even ones specially designed to undo adhesives and epoxies. These do remove a great variety of stubborn soils, and at least the solvents in them are carefully chosen and buffered. The ones without pumice are easier on the epidermis.

Almost all cleaning is hard on the hands, with all the strong solutions, hot and cold water, rubbing, and scrubbing it gets them involved in. So after the last sponge is squeezed dry and the last bucket emptied, treat your only two irreplaceable tools to a little moisturizing massage with lanolin or hand cream.

Anything special I need to know about cleaning a microwave oven ? #76

The media have credited me with saving millions of hours of housework around the world, but I'm not even close to the real unsung hero of kitchen cleanup. The mild-mannered microwave oven, now in 75 percent of American homes, eliminates millions of hard-to-clean pots and pans and tons of airborne cooking grease every single day. But best of all, we can now say "Clean the oven" with a smile.

Since the interior of a microwave oven stays relatively cool during cooking, we don't get those burned puddles of pie filling and petrified pizza cheese that mar the insides of conventional ovens. Most of what gets on the inside of a microwave can be wiped off with a damp cloth or paper towel as long as you catch it right away. If you just get in the habit of wiping out your microwave every time you use it, you shouldn't ever have to do any scrubbing. Just use a dishcloth dipped in clean dishwater like you do on the countertops and stove. Do the roof of the oven, too.

It's hard to see, so it's easy to forget. If your oven has a removable tray on the bottom, take it out and wash it in the sink or the dishwasher every once in a while. You want to clean the rubber gaskets around the door and the area right around them fairly often also, and for that matter, the whole inside of the oven door. It'll help assure that those mysterious microwaves stay safely sealed inside.

When you slick up the outside of your oven, just use a slightly damp cloth—you especially don't want to get any excess water on the control panel. Then polish with a clean, dry towel. Always touch "clear" after you clean the panel to prevent a case of cleaned-on instructions. Vacuum out the dust vents from time to time, too, and don't pile stuff on top of or against them. Some ovens have surfaces or optional features that require special care, so do sit down sometime soon and actually **read** the little booklet that came with your oven, which includes the manufacturer's directions for cleaning.

Should an egg or an Idaho potato explode inside a microwave and you happen to leave it all on there to dry out and harden, it's still no sweat. Just put a half cup of water in the oven and let it boil for a few minutes; the steam will soften any dried-on stuff and make it easy to remove. For really tough spots you may need to scrub a little with a white nylon-backed scrub sponge. Just remember that many microwave parts are made of plastic—even the windows on some models—so don't use metal scrapers, steel wool, powdered cleaners, or harsh cleaning products that could scratch and damage. After what I've been telling you for six books now, you should't have any of this stuff around the house anyhow. And never, ever use oven cleaner in a microwave—it's way too strong!

Since microwaves don't get hot enough to kill all the bacteria, crumbs and spills left behind can cause odors. Keeping your oven clean is the obvious answer to odors, but you can also try wiping it out with a solution of four tablespoons of baking soda in a quart of warm water. Some people like to boil a little lemon and cloves or pumpkin pie spice mix in a bowl of water in there to keep their "mike" smelling good, but everyone will hate you when they find out it isn't a pie baking.

Whatever you do, take good care of that little rascal; it's probably saving you over two hundred hours of cooking and cleaning time a year!

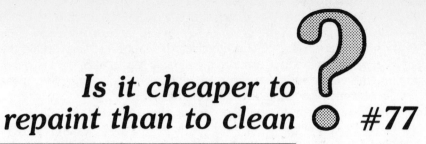

Is it cheaper to repaint than to clean ❓ *#77*

Where did the doctrine of painting to solve cleaning problems originate anyway? In a congregation that was painting a church instead of cleaning it like they should have. They only had half as much paint as they needed, so to make it stretch they kept adding thinner, which of course did a crummy job on the church. As they packed their equipment to leave, the earth shook, the sky thundered, and a mighty voice came out of the heavens: "Repaint, you thinners!"

Homemakers have been religiously repainting ever since, because it's allegedly easier than cleaning. But that's definitely not so! Painting is at least 85 percent harder and more expensive than cleaning. I've been a licensed paint contractor for more than twenty-five years, and even though I know how to do it fast and easy, it's still not the way to go when a simple cleaning will do. Would you dye a dirty carpet rather than clean it? On the other hand, if the surface is worn, damaged, out of style, impossible to clean, or needs protection, painting is an acceptable, even intelligent solution.

Sure, painting has pizzazz, but it also has preparation—priming, filling holes, patching, sanding, spackling, covering, masking, cleanup, and . . . need I go on? If it's merely dirty, painting isn't just a waste of time and money; it creates future maintenance problems. Paint has weight and mass; it doesn't just change the color—every time the Eiffel Tower in France is painted it adds twenty thousand pounds! Paint is like the frosting on a cake—just the right amount is great and earns applause, but too much ruins it. Look at beautiful new woodwork, how keen and pronounced all the carvings and corners and edges are. Twelve coats of paint later, they look gobbed up, dripped on, rounded, and kind of apartment-house cheap and tacky. Look at baseboards—we all paint them a lot, and then when they get a chip knocked in them it looks like a miniature Grand Canyon.

Painting "instead" of cleaning is a fallacy anyway, because thoroughly cleaning the surface is an essential part of good preparation for painting. If you paint over dirt, you're just asking for poor coverage and weak adhesion.

If you have grease- and dirt-embedded flat latex paint and it won't clean up well, paint it. But the same situation on enamel paint can be cleaned up in minutes, leaving the surface almost as good as new. If most of the paint is in good shape with the exception of a few chips or nail holes, touch them up with a little spackle and a dab of paint on a cotton swab; don't repaint the whole thing! Keeping a baby food jar of each color you use when you paint—**and labeling the jar!**—and just touching up as needed can almost double the life of a paint job.

And when you do paint, remember that you want to clean, not repaint, for the next five to ten years, so buy good, cleanable paint. It might cost a few more dollars a gallon, but it'll save you twenty gallons worth of unnecessary premature repainting. For maximum cleanability I like to stick with the best grade of the major brands and use a semigloss enamel or even a gloss in ultra-high-abuse areas like exterior doors and door frames and use eggshell or satin enamel wherever I want a lower luster.

What's the best metal polish  *#78*

We all ask this question the minute we find out that spit and a quick rub on our shirt sleeve just doesn't cut it. With polished gold leading the list and from there right on down to a tin bucket, metal looks its best when it's bright and shiny. Soap and water and a little muscle will clean most metal—remove the surface dirt and grime— but it can never make metal look magnificent, especially the tarnishing types like copper, silver, and brass. It takes a metal polish to do that—something we've all used at one time or another on candlesticks, car bumpers, brass railings, and other ornamental stuff. The "polish" is generally a creamy solvent-smelling liquid, which we pour onto a cloth and slather over the subject. Then we give it a little rubdown, let it dry, and start briskly brandishing our polishing cloth. As the cloth gets blacker, the metal gets brighter, and we repeat the whole process until it shines enough to make **us** glow with pride. This process works a lot better than home remedies like baking soda, lemons, salt, and vinegar, but it is slow and messy. My army uniform always got more polish on it than the brass buttons did.

There's been an improvement in these all-purpose metal polishes that makes them a little easier to use. Basically this same mixture of solvent, oil, and light abrasive is now impregnated into a soft cotton "rope" and wound down into a can. You simply open the lid and tear off a hunk to match the task at hand and rub the metal with it. No pouring, no spills, no rummaging around for a rag—just instant ready-to-go metal polish in a can. After rubbing with your polishing rope, you just buff the object to a rich shine with a soft, clean cloth. I love it—the can has about seven feet of metal polish in it (imagine measuring metal polish in feet instead of ounces!), and when the cotton is totally black, if the piece isn't pretty enough, tear another little hunk off and give it that final gleam. Then just chuck the used piece and put the lid back on the can.

This rope dope is clear, not chalky and opaque like the liquid polishes, so you don't end up with whitish powdery gunk down in the grooves and indentations of the object where it's hard to remove. And with a piece of polish rope you have much better control of where the polish goes, so you're a lot less likely to end up with it all over surrounding or adjoining surfaces. You can find my favorite brand of this type of polish—Ouater (pronounced *water)*—in hardware stores.

There's also a new creamy polish called Flitz that does an above-average job on many metals. But no matter what it says on the label, don't expect any one product to work equally well on all metals. All-purpose, in metal polish as in anything, means a compromise between what each particular thing really needs. Most all-purpose polishes are too scratchy for silver and chrome and not very effective on aluminum, copper, or stainless steel. The best bets for these metals are still the specialized products formulated specifically for each metal, i.e., silver polish for silver, copper cleaner for copper, chrome polish for chrome, etc.

A few last pointers for metal polishers: All metal polishes contain abrasives, because the way they get things shiny is by "sanding" away the dull coat of oxide or tarnish on the surface. An object is actually a little thinner every time you take a polish rag to it. So don't overdo it—rub only as hard as needed to remove the tarnish and be especially careful on plated metal so you don't polish your way down to pot metal. And you usually don't want to use metal polish on lacquered or antique or satin finishes.

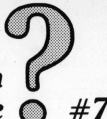

How do I clean leather furniture #79

As long as it's inside and out of the weather, leather stays nice indefinitely, but it does get dirty! You can tell leather is in need of cleaning when it gets dull and discolored-looking and you begin to see gunge spots on it. I'm talking about finished leather—with a smooth, dyed surface—not suede. Suede or "rough" leather has no protective finish and will absorb every stain. Beyond brushing it with a suede brush, I'd leave suede cleaning to the pros.

The gentle cleaner preferred by those who have cleaned finished leather for decades is old reliable saddle soap. Before you soap, dust off the surface and vacuum or brush out any dirt trapped around the buttons or in tucks and corners. With a sponge dipped in water and squeezed almost dry, work up a head of suds in the tin of saddle soap. Apply the lather to the surface of the furniture, rubbing east to west and

186

north to south, and the dirt will come foaming off. Carefully clean around the buttons, any piping, and in tucks, welts and creases, too. Places like these collect the worst stuff, so work the soap in and under here and give the crevices a swipe or two with a soft toothbrush. Go very gently—with scarcely any soap or pressure—over any areas with gold tooling or decoration. Then with a clean cloth lightly moistened with clear water and wrung out rinse the dirt and soap away. **Water won't hurt leather if used quickly**—just don't let it stand or puddle on there. Do a section at a time—the pros do the seat first, the backrest next, and the sides and the back of the whole piece last. Then buff with a dry cloth. Be sure to let the furniture dry completely before putting it back in use so nothing will come off on your clothes.

If the leather is in fair shape this should do it. The little bit of saddle soap that works into the grain of the leather will help to preserve it and keep it supple. But if the leather is getting dry and showing cracks or stress points, you need to clean it as described and then rub in a generous coat of one of the many leather conditioners on the market. You probably won't want to use neatsfoot oil, because it leaves a matte finish behind. Many leather conditioners will darken leather, too, so if you have a white or light-colored piece use white Vaseline instead or make sure the conditioner you use is a type suitable for use on light surfaces. Work the conditioner in all over and then wipe off any excess—this should get your leather back to soft and luxurious.

Leather's enemies are water, sunlight, and heat, which dry, stiffen, shrink, and crack it. But if you treat it right, leather will last forever. Jim Abdo of Omaha, one of the real specialists in the furniture cleaning business, has been taking care of one client's leather furniture for several decades, and it still looks brand new. He recommends cleaning leather annually. If you're not sure whether a particular piece really is leather—some textured vinyl fabrics would even fool a mother cow—look under the furniture and find a tucked edge and you can tell. If you do happen to clean vinyl with saddle soap, that won't hurt a thing, so if in doubt, use the soap. Don't use waxes or furniture polish on leather, though—the solvents in these will soften and damage the finish.

What's the best way to clean a barbecue 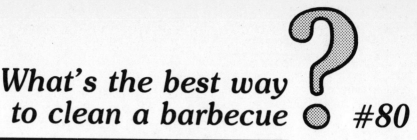 #80

At scout camp back in 1947 I washed all the dishes and when I got to the troop cooking grill it seemed to be caked with crud, so I sanded it down to the bare metal with steel wool, creek sand, and my scout knife. Then I proudly presented it to our seasoned outdoorsman scoutmaster and his face turned whiter than the shining steel. "You ruined it, you idiot. It took twenty years to build the cooking carbon on that grill, and you ruined it!"

I tell this tale just to remind us that grill and barbecue scouring is one form of cleaning where you don't necessarily want to remove every last

188

little bit of buildup on there, the cooking surface proper, that is. A good dark layer of carbon "seasoning" is nothing less than sacred to real barbecue buffs because it helps the grill heat more evenly and keeps meat from sticking to the metal.

So when it comes to the actual cooking grill, or grate—which gets sterilized by fire rather regularly—all you really have to do is get rid of the excess crustness on there with a few brisk rubs with a brass wire brush or stainless steel pad. The best time to quick-clean your grill like this—if you can manage to forsake the barbecued ribs for a few minutes—is right after cooking, while it's still warm (not hot!) and the grease is still soft.

If it's plated or stainless steel grill and you insist on seeing it shiny or the layers of cremated steak grease have accumulated to the point where your steak's riding high out of the fire, you can scrub your way all the way down to the wire, but why bother? Much better to let time and the right chemical do it for you. This means, as long as it's not aluminum, just spray it all over on both sides with oven cleaner, slip it into a plastic garbage bag, and put it somewhere well away from small children for several hours or overnight. Or soak it in a good, strong solution of heavy-duty household cleaner like Top Job or a degreaser for several hours or overnight. Either way, the incrustations should slide right off.

Coating the freshly cleaned grill with cooking oil, such as peanut oil, after it's dry will help keep rust away and keep stuff from collecting as quickly this time. A cast iron grill you always want to reoil after scraping or cleaning.

If that cooking grill just drops into a humble cast iron or steel **hibachi**, all you have to do is dump the ashes every once in a while, scrape, scrub, or brush off any spills or stuck-on stuff inside or out, and give the whole thing a thin coat of oil when you're through.

If it's a **kettle grill** that's perched on your patio, you can use oven cleaner with impunity on any of the inside surfaces, but keep it off the outside. Keep scrapers and metal scrubbers off the painted outside, too, and oven cleaner 100 percent away from aluminum parts and accessories— or they'll be a sad whitened, pitted sight. And never try to do any cleaning or hosing of anything before the whole kettle is good and cool. Hardened deposits usually only develop around the upper inside walls of the bowl; otherwise a quick wipe inside and out with warm detergent water, then a dry paper towel should keep your kettle happy.

If it's a **gas grill** that decorates your deck, I'm sure you're pleased to know these babies are at least partially self-cleaning. When you're done cooking you just close the hood and crank the heat up to high for fifteen or twenty minutes and char off anything left on there. When the grill cools, all you have to wipe away are a few ash particles. To keep this piece of combustion-regulating machinery running smoothly and safely, though, there's a couple little cleaning operations you'd better not neglect or postpone. Your owner's manual will tell you exactly what they are and how to do them, but in general it involves checking and cleaning venturi tubes, valve orifice, and pressure regulator vents. The venturi tubes are a special problem because spiders and wasps love to crawl in them and make themselves comfortable. The resulting blockage won't just foul up the heating flame—it can cause a fuel backup and *fire*.

Once a year or so, make sure it's **off** and give the whole grill a going over. You don't want to use oven cleaner anyplace here but on porcelain grill surfaces, because the "bodies" of gas grills are usually cast or anodized aluminum. Keep powdered cleansers, abrasive pads, and strong degreasers away from any painted or nonstick surfaces, too.

If the rocks are removable, boil them in dish detergent solution; flavorizer bars can be cleaned with a brass-wire brush or even run through the dishwasher. Hit the burner with hot detergent solution or a wire brush if need be to get rid of hardened spills or rust. Unclog the burner holes with a thin wire or opened paper clip while you're at it, being **very** careful not to make them any bigger in the process.

When you've removed everything removable, clean the inside of the grill with a stiff brush and detergent solution and a wet scraper for bad spots. You'll want to tape the gas openings closed first to keep out any water. Then run a damp sponge over the outside and give the whole grill a hose rinsing. When the grill is good and dry, oil any wooden parts with boiled linseed oil to keep them from cracking.

To help speed cleaning next time, you can spray the inside of the grill with a nonstick grill or cooking spray when you're finished or line the bottom with heavy-duty foil, as long as you make holes in it to allow the grill's air vents to function.

P.S. You'll have a lot less flareup (and cleanup) if you trim that excess artery-clogging fat off food and make sure the grease drain in your grill isn't clogged up either.

. . . (the one in the house, not the one in my head)

Where there's a party, there will be a mess. You can count on it. The very word *party* instantly clears people's minds of anything resembling responsibility. The last thing partiers want is to be neat and orderly. So it's up to us to remember the mess is imminent and *prepare!*

Plan the festivities for a part of the house with expendable furniture and fairly durable surfaces. Stifle the urge to show off: stay out of rooms packed with your prized possessions. Weather permitting, outside parties are a lot easier on the interior decoration, even if it will mean making a few provisions for wind or rain and a few napkins blowing over to the neighbors'.

• To keep down cigarette burns, one of the big hazards of party giving, set out tastefully lettered "no smoking" signs or designate a single area such as a porch for the purpose.

• Provide plenty of trash receptacles. If a partier needs to get rid of something and there's no waste can in sight, it'll end up on the window-sill or under a cushion.

• If it's a children's party, make your little visitors surrender their Double Bubble at the door and under no circumstances include any in the favors. Serve all food on a hard-surface floor; make the tables and chairs their size (reaching only leads to tipping and spilling); make sure you use paper everything.

Food, of course, has phenomenal mess potential, so let's start thinking in terms of a low-mess menu. How we serve has a lot to do with it, and buffet is about the worst. Offering food this way is coming right out and asking people to walk all over the house with it. Where there is carrying and moving around and balancing of plates on knees there will be dropping and spilling and smearing. Plus in the case of a buffet, a lot of excess food lying around because they took a serving or two extra side dishes more than they could handle.

Far better to have all the eating done in one place at one time on the surface actually designed for it—a table. If you must serve elsewhere, make everyone sit down first and bring the food to them and provide some surface a lot steadier than the human lap to set things on.

As for *what* to serve, the guidelines here are pretty obvious:

• Nothing that's messy to prepare *and* to eat, such as deviled eggs.

• Nothing that will result in bones, pits, shells, or peelings to be left all over.

• Nothing round, like peas or grapes, that can roll away to be smashed into the floor or carpet. Unsteady cylinders like corn on the cob are out, too.

• Nothing in tiny individual wrappers or on toothpicks unless you get good enough with a Chinese cleaver to make edible ones.

• Nothing you have to lean or bend over to eat or that call for the use of chopsticks. Forget about fondue, too.

• Nothing red or orange, especially barbecue or spaghetti.

• No recipe that involves sauce, topping, or frosting and only clear soups—no creamy anything.

• Nothing crumbly or crusty or oily—chips and dips are out on at least two counts here—and nothing that people grab in handfuls.

What can you serve? A one-inch cube of clear gelatin can be served safely at most gatherings. You're also fairly safe with finger foods that aren't greasy or little finger sandwiches with the crusts trimmed off and filled with something that doesn't glop out easily. Or something that looks good but no one will actually want to eat or even pick up, preferably. If you succeed in the latter, it can double as a centerpiece.

As for beverages, the other half of the battle, how you serve it is as critical as what you serve. Consider only cork-bottomed trays or trays with a secure lip—not the "ski-jump" style with an upfluted edge that only gives a sliding glass extra impetus. A cart with well-lipped shelves is better yet to serve or clean up from—there's lots of nice, stable storage or serving space, and no one can fail to notice you coming and going. To reduce those white rings on furniture surfaces provide plenty of coasters, and **paper** cups, which are less prone to the condensation that often causes this problem. You could also serve in paper cones—it's impossible to set them down anywhere.

Otherwise you can:

• Serve all hot beverages in nontip commuter mugs

• Replace the old punch bowl, ladle, and awkward little cups with the astronauts' choice: Tang in clear plastic squeeze pouches. Or contact your local fast-food chain for a supply of plastic cups and lids with the little holes in the middle for straws.

• Serve nothing cherry or grape flavored and white wine only.

• Offer no drinks that involve fruit slices, cherries, pineapple chunks, or stirrers.

• If there weren't any ice cubes there wouldn't be an inch or so of water in all the glasses everyone leaves around everywhere.

When it comes to **decorations**, remember that what goes up must come down. Don't forget that crepe paper stains when it's wet and tape goes on a lot easier than it comes off. Don't even consider confetti. For showers, birthdays, and other present getting parties try to figure out an unwrapping routine that doesn't end up with a floorful of crumpled paper and scattered ribbons. Or at least have a spotter to retrieve and trash.

Finally, don't leave it all for the morning. No matter how beat you are, try to at least get all the spills up and precariously placed things put away before you collapse—most stains only set and worsen with time.

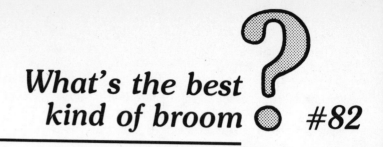

One with a willing arm attached to the handle! Any broom will work, but the one that will do the most, the best, and the easiest is the one we all want. The new angle brooms with the exploded tip nylon bristles are my favorite. They do a fine job on the "big stuff," but they also get all the fine dust and dirt, in fewer broom strokes. They're light and easy to handle and much more adept at reaching under cabinets and into corners. Moisture and chemicals, which can cause the slow death of corn brooms, won't bother them—since they don't absorb anything, they won't mold or mildew like a corn broom that's gone wading. And unlike the old Martha Washington special, they don't shed all over shamelessly.

194

Best of all, when you use an angle broom, you're not just sweeping with part of the broom. Our natural sweeping stroke has any broom hitting the floor at an angle, and if the broom is angled, too, at least we have the whole head coming in contact with the floor.

I'd give a sweeping vote of confidence to the Rubbermaid professional model 2021 or the Hoky Smart Broom. The only disadvantage of these brooms is that under the right, or wrong, conditions, when you leave them standing for a while the bristles warp into a rather obtuse angle, so hang them up! You ought to be doing that with all your brooms anyway. Corn brooms will lean out of shape too, but unlike their plastic counterparts, a brief dunk in hot water or a rubber-band-around-the-bristles reshaping period won't bring them around.

If you can't bear to be without a corn broom, be advised that most of the grocery store models are too scrawny—one with a nine- or ten-inch head is what you really want. And corn brooms do benefit from an occasional sprinkle of clean water to keep the bristles from getting brittle.

For the garage, driveway, patio, and sidewalk, a push broom with a twenty-four-inch head is an excellent addition to the broom closet. A good push broom can move dirt, leaves, sawdust, grass clippings, and light accumulations of snow in record time. The best kind has nylon bristles, which again are unaffected by water and chemicals. There's an inner core of coarse bristles that give the broom the bite and muscle to move heavy gravel and the like and to scrub loose things like dried-on soil. A ring of finer bristles around the outside catches any small particles and dust missed by the center section. A handle brace is a good thing to have on there, too, to stabilize the head and prevent wobbling and broken handles.

What about imprints and stains in the carpet from furniture ❓ *#83*

This is always good for a gasp of horror—when you move a piece of furniture and there in the carpet are four rusty ruts! Or mahogany-stained ruts! Or just plain ruts! The rust got there because you put the furniture back on a damp or wet carpet after cleaning—the metal "shoes" (furniture glides) on the bottom of the legs did it. The mahogany or other tint is also from the bottom of the leg, where the stained wood usually isn't protected with varnish. When exposed to moisture, this coloring can bleed onto the carpet. The plain old impression is just crushed pile.

For rust stains use a rust remover from a janitorial-supply store, then rinse with water and blot. Be sure to read the instructions on the label and **follow** them, because professional-quality rust removers are very effective but also potentially very dangerous. For wood stain try blotting with alcohol first, then dry cleaning solvent, then lacquer thinner, if necessary. Pretest these procedures in an inconspicuous area first. Finish up with a mild detergent solution and then a water rinse. Migrated dyes from the wood may be impossible to remove—if the steps suggested above are unsuccessful, consult a pro carpet cleaner.

As for those plain old depressions, they can usually be popped back up as follows: rub the tufts upright with a coin. Rub, don't frizz them! Then steam the area by holding your steam iron just above the carpet—be careful not to actually touch the carpet, or you might melt it. Sometimes just a little hot water rubbed on with a cloth will stand the tufts back up, too. Don't steam until after you've removed any stains, or the steam may set them.

To prevent this: A piece of unprinted cardboard or sandwich bag inserted under each furniture leg when you shampoo the carpet will do the trick. Leave these little guards in place until the carpet is good and dry. Moving furniture an inch or so each time you vacuum will keep indentations from becoming permanent. Rubber or plastic coasters under the legs help, too.

I've taught a lot of you, in the last ten years, how to do a streak-free job on glass with a squeegee the fast, professional way. But what about the frame and sill and tracks, which also accumulate a lot of grime?

The mistake most of us make here is to work like mad to get the glass clean and then try to clean the rest of the window. So of course all that dust and sand, all those paint flakes and putty chips and moth and beetle bodies, quickly muck up our masterpiece. We may just quietly decide to ignore the rest of the window to avoid smearing up our sparkling panes.

It took me a while to figure out the obvious answer: **Before** starting on the glass, wash down the frame, sill, track, etc. Use the same harmless, mild solution of dish soap in water you use on the window itself—ten drops of detergent to a gallon of water—and apply it with a sponge or brush. If you're working outside, spray the frames off forcefully with a hose before you start to blast away stray leaves and bird droppings and dried mud and the like. Then you can just flood the frame and edges with the solution and let it run right off; it won't hurt the house or plants or anything. You'll have to be more conservative on the inside. First, scrape loose and vacuum out the dead insects and impacted crud in the window tracks—this stuff is an incredible mess once it gets wet. Then when you wet down the frame let the solution run down into the tracks and sit there a minute or two to soften any remaining gunk. What won't come off with a white nylon-backed scrub sponge after that scrape out with a putty knife or a screwdriver covered with a towel—it's just the right size to swoop right down a track. I always wipe the frame down next, so that all that side dirt that would get under your squeegee blade and mess up the glass is flushed away.

Just be sure to let the solution soak awhile, and it'll dissolve most of the dirt by itself—that's the key to easy removal.

If you have screens, hose them down good, spraying vigorously from both sides to break loose any debris, then let them drip dry before reinstalling. If they're extra-dirty apply some of your window-cleaning solution with a soft bristle brush before you hose.

You don't have to do a full-scale renovation on the frames every time you do the glass—I'll bet if you only cleaned the rest of the window once a year the windowsill inspection committee would rest easier.

What is Corian, and is it easier to maintain than cultured marble or Formica 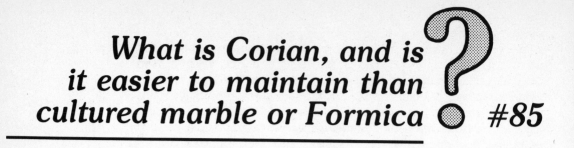 #85

Corian is the new kid on the block, or should we say on the kitchen counter, the bathroom vanity, and lots of other important places. It's good stuff—my wife and I had it installed in our guest house in Hawaii and are putting it in the maintenance-free house we're building there, too. After living with it for a year or two, I liked it so well I used it for the sinks and vanities of my new business headquarters and Cleaning Center store, too.

Corian is a unique material from DuPont, a strong acrylic formed into sheets under high pressure, and it's the same all the way through, not just a surface veneer like plastic laminates. This means you'll never scrub the pattern off and minor nicks, cuts, and burns can even be sanded out and removed. It resists scuffing and staining and won't provide a home for mold or mildew the way grouted tile does. It actually thrives on

200

cleaning with powdered cleanser, which will dull and ruin plastic laminates, cultured marble, and fiberglass. It's tough but satiny smooth and subtly elegant, as well as warm and pleasing to the touch.

We beat our countertops hard in Hawaii, plunking pineapples and cracking coconuts on them, and Corian can take all that abuse and all those tough island fruits and still look like a queen's dressing table. It comes in several decorator colors and three thicknesses, with molded-in sinks if desired. I use quarter-inch Corian for places like shower walls and a half to three-quarter inch thickness on counters or spans that need the extra support. Corian can be cut and worked like wood, so you can even create your own custom designs with it. Sounds too good to be true, you say? There has to be a hitch?

O.K., it does cost more initially. But you'll save on maintenance costs and cleaning effort for the lifetime of the installation. I'm not a luxury buyer but a practical one, and getting something that's attractive, incredibly durable, and resists damage and stains forever is worth it in my book. And it costs less to install Corian than that other mess-resistant and enduring surface, ceramic tile.

You aren't likely to find Corian at your local do-it-yourself store—so check out kitchen cabinet shops or ask the builder, architect, or contractor about it if you're drafting your dream house or remodeling.

Corian's primary use is countertops and tub/shower enclosures, but I've seen it used for walls, signs, windowsills, baseboards, thresholds, shelving, desktops, tabletops, bank teller counters, planters, banisters, bathroom stalls, and—thank the Lord for real brilliance—even waste containers.

Is there any way to keep down the mess from a wood-burning stove ❓ ⬤ #86

We all think immediately of ashes and soot, but no minor part of the mess from a wood-burning stove is the wood itself and our heavy-handed handling of it. Our ancestors all burned wood, but they weren't as vain about it as we are. We pile the wood up as high as humanly possible for rustic effect and then grab and haul it in by the brawny armful—a process that snags our sweater or puts pitch stains on our shirt. It also scatters bark, twigs, splinters, chips, and bugs from porch, backyard, or shed to house door and then stove door and a ten-foot-square area around the indoor woodpile.

Back in the old "clean stove days," no one would be caught without a woodbox to contain and confine the mess. Smart people not only have a woodbox, but a little hand truck to take it out, fill it, and bring it back in—without a drop of debris. You can easily pound together a woodbox out of plywood and paint, stain, or varnish it. You may even

202

want to add a lid with a cushion or bit of carpeting on it, so you can sit by the fire and swap stories or warm your toes.

If your woodbox is too big to be dollied in and out, get a canvas or nylon log carrier—mail order catalogs love to offer these—to keep down the forestry fallout. As for the woodpile itself, forget about whether or not your pretty piles can be viewed to advantage by passersby and put the woodpile somewhere protected from the elements where a little mess won't matter. Woodpiles do nothing to dress up a front porch and attract and harbor wee beasties of all kinds in range of the front door. A woodpile should ideally be on a wood rack well up off the ground, so the logs won't rot and crumble and get insect-infested and muddy your clothing when you handle them. It doesn't hurt, either, to try to buy or gather wood that looks clean and insect-free to begin with, and try for the less shaggy types, like tight-barked maple, birch, or beech. A pair of sturdy tongs will make it possible to insert a log neatly, rather than fling it into the fire, scattering ashes and sparks everywhere.

As for those ashes:

• If at all possible, go for a stove model with an ash drawer, so you can just slide that drawer out gently and dump it into a metal bin.

• If yours doesn't have a drawer, spread some newspapers before you start shoveling. I promise you'll spill.

• For this very reason as well as to catch log fallout, a little hand vacuum mounted on the wall near the stove makes excellent sense.

• Get yourself a good fireproof ash bucket with a lid. If you have a decent tool for the job, you'll be less likely to put it off indefinitely. And the lid will help keep flyaway ashes down.

• Carefully scoop those ashes out; don't sling or toss them.

• To ease the inevitable cleanup after ash removal, the surface around and under your stove or the hearth in front of it should be a smooth, easily sweepable surface. Ceramic tile or smooth, sealed stone—not rough brick or craggy rock with quarter-inch deep mortar joints.

To keep your walls and ceilings unbesooted, be sure all stovepipe seams are well sealed and always open the chimney damper, if there is one, before you open the stove door. If you start a fire with the damper closed, all that smoke goes out the door instead of up the chimney!

It's also important to have the flue cleaned out annually, preferably by a professional. This prevents creosote buildup, which is not only a fire risk, but blocks the air passageway (flue) and ups the smoke quotient. And when you do get a slight smoke accumulation on the wall use a dry sponge on it (see p. 219).

P.S. Porcelain finishes aren't just elegant—they don't have to be treated with stove polish that will always come off on your hands.

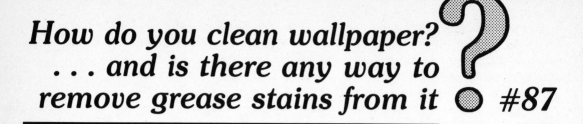

How do you clean wallpaper? ... and is there any way to remove grease stains from it ● *#87*

The "paper" in wallpaper is or should be a thing of the past. "Wall covering" is the new description of those rolls of prints, patterns, and hues that have dressed up our vertical surfaces for centuries. The old paper was exactly that: fragile, absorbent paper—hard to install, easy to tear or stain, and impossible to clean. The popularity of paper in kitchens and its lack of durability there stimulated the development of the stain- and splash-resistant vinyls. These are coated or impregnated with plastic, so they're rugged, hard to stain or tear, and much easier to clean. They come in various grades of washability: "washable," which withstands water used sparingly but no scrubbing, and "scrubbable," which means you can rub and scrub a bit, but don't pull out all the

204

scour-power stops. If you're not sure what you have, do a little gentle scrubbing with a damp cloth in an inconspicuous place or, better yet, on a saved wallpaper scrap, should you be in the giddy position of remembering where they're stashed. If it makes a dark, wet spot, loosens the adhesive, causes dye to run or fade, or the pattern wipes right off, you'll know how far you can go out in the visible areas.

The newer solid vinyl, fabric-backed vinyl, or vinyl-covered paper wall coverings can be given an overall cleaning with a mild solution of neutral cleaner, much like a painted wall—but don't flood the seams or rub across them—wipe seams the long way. Wipe the solution on with a damp sponge—this is one place **not** to let the solution soak, especially on the seams—then dry the area with a clean terry towel, always working top to bottom.

What flocked papers mainly need by way of cleaning is not washing but an occasional dry-brushing or vacuuming.

Whenever I have to clean the old-type wallpaper—on which no water should ever be used—I do it with something called a dry sponge, a five-by-seven-inch pad of virgin rubber about half an inch thick. It removes dry dirt from paper better than anything I know—just like a giant eraser. An art gum eraser or one of the dough type wallpaper cleaners can be used for isolated smudges, but it's not nearly as effective as a dry sponge for cleaning large areas.

To dry sponge, dust the wall first with a clean, untreated dust mop or, better yet, the dusting brush on a cannister vac. This will head off streaks from cobwebs or loose surface dirt. Then fold the dry sponge in half and wipe your way over the paper in straight, overlapping strokes. When your sponge begins to get grimy, fold it over to a fresh surface and swipe on.

As for those grease stains, most of the new wall coverings are stainproof to a degree and can be gently spot cleaned with a solvent spotter like K2r. For stubborn spots of crayon or wax try gently rubbing with a dry steel wool pad, followed by dry cleaning solvent. Abrasive cleaners should only be used as a last resort—and never on foil—as they're all too likely to remove the pattern as well as the spot. For stains like ink and marker you may have to patch in a new piece of paper—most solvents that would remove the stain will also remove the dye from the paper. In all spot cleaning on paper beware of the "bright spot" effect—getting the stain out, but ending up with a single very clean spot that stands out strikingly from the rest of the paper.

There are clear protective coatings available that make marginally washable wallcoverings more stain resistant and scrubbable—check with a wallpaper store. Or you could carefully repeat that strained beets splotch every twenty inches.

Is there any way to get rid of water stains on ceilings ❓ #88

Sure! Have you ever noticed that when you hear some people say their roof leaked you and others slyly glance upward and . . . no stain! They removed it? Indeed they did. I became an expert ceiling stain remover when I owned a mobile home. All mobile homes get roof leaks and leaks account for about 95 percent of ceiling stains. Water or roof seepage of some kind works its way through the roofing material, the rafters, and the insulation, picking up color as it goes. Finally it soaks through the ceiling and leaves a brownish-yellow (sepia!) stain or line. We have a hard time with this because it's not a mark that you can simply clean off—the ceiling material has actually been dyed. In areas of high humidity, black mildew specks may also grow on top of the spot.

Whether or not you can successfully remove it does depend on the severity of the stain. If the spot has gotten really wet, there's always swelling and some disintegration of the ceiling sheetrock or tile, so poke the area with your finger and make sure it's solid and not just suspended mush. If it's the latter, replace it now—don't think you're going to hold it together with paint.

For a slight stain you can often blot or spray on a little bleach—one part chlorine bleach such as Clorox to five parts water, or undiluted hydrogen peroxide—assuming the ceiling is white, which most are. This will usually oxidize and whiten it. It can't hurt to try this first—most of the new acoustic ceiling cleaning solutions being used by professionals today to restore dirty or stained ceilings are bleachlike products. If you're up against mildew, too, the chlorine bleach solution will kill it and lighten the stain at the same time.

If the stain is just small droplets or a little line, a dab of white shoe polish or touch up paint on a cotton swab will at least keep it from being the first thing people see when they step into the room.

The best approach for a larger stain—and it's easy—is to buy some pigmented shellac and brush it over the stained area to prevent any further seepage. Then after it dries simply roll or brush some matching paint on the area, stopping at the seam lines or feathering the edges, if you don't want to paint the whole ceiling. If you don't shellac it first, that stain will bleed through sixteen coats of paint. Easier yet, spray cans of acoustic ceiling touch-up paint are available now in off-white shades that match most acoustic tiles and require no priming or sealing.

P.S. Fix the leak and give the ceiling a chance to dry out well before proceeding with any of these directions!

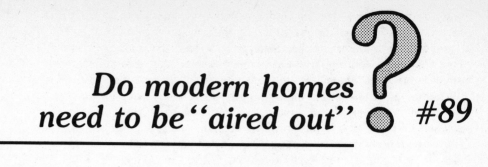

Do modern homes need to be "aired out"? #89

Today's homes actually need airing out even more than Grandma's did, but the practice has gone out of style. In Grandma's day, "airing out" was an announcement of the arrival of warmer weather. The house, which had been draft-proofed as far as possible with storm windows, heavy curtains, felt strips around the door and window frames, and blankets stuffed under the doors, was opened up to let the fresh spring breezes flow through. And as winter's pent up cooking and heating odors wafted away on the wind, serious spring cleaning began.

But talk about tightly closed up! Our modern homes make those of

208

thirty or forty years ago seem like wind tunnels by comparison. You can almost feel your ears pop when you slam the door. Constant little drafts drifted into Grandma's house, through the keyholes and the cracks around the windows, up from the cellar and from under the kitchen cabinets, and down the chimney. Our homes today are sealed up so snug with vapor barriers, improved insulation, double-glazed windows, high-efficiency weatherstripping, and lifetime caulk that very few vagrant breezes find their way in. And we seldom open the windows anymore, because we're either heating, cooling, filtering, or humidifying the inside air and we wouldn't dare crack a door or window too long for fear of wasting precious energy or that the cat or the cockatoo would escape.

Our new homes and buildings have coined the phrase *indoor air pollution* to try to describe what it's like to be trapped inside a relatively airtight structure with an atmosphere full of toxic substances and not enough fresh air exchange from outside. The pollutants range from cigarette smoke and carbon monoxide to sulfur dioxide and mold spores. They come from our appliances and heating devices, our paints and arts and craft supplies, our cosmetics and grooming products, and our cleaning and pest control preparations, especially the aerosol ones. Many building and furnishing materials, too, exude harmful fumes: The resins and solvents in particle board subfloors, certain wallboards, carpeting, and a variety of mastics and adhesives put formaldehyde and other noxious vapors into the indoor air. The colorless, odorless gas called radon, for example, a natural byproduct of uranium decomposition, seeps into our homes from the soil beneath.

At the office or at home, we spend three quarters or more of our time inside these days. And believe it or not, the outside air in even the most polluted city is better for us than most air indoors. We do have furnaces and air conditioners that move the air around a little, but they don't bring in any new air—just the same old stale air back again, in a choice of heated or chilled. In modern commercial buildings, where windows rarely open and the indoor air for all practical purposes doesn't exchange with fresh outdoor air at all, indoor pollution is a serious matter indeed.

What does indoor pollution do? It stains and damages and shortens the life of our possessions and furnishings. It gives us coughs and sneezes and stuffy noses, irritates our eyes and throat and skin, aggravates our asthma or allergies or bronchitis, and makes us listless or nauseous or "tired." So when Mom said, "Go outside and get some fresh air," she wasn't so far off, was she?

What can we do about all this? We can test for radon, carbon monoxide, and certain other pollutants and take measures to reduce their concentration in our home. If you think you might have an indoor pollution problem, you can get information on testing from your county health department or from your regional office of the Environmental

Protection Agency. Testing is a smart thing to do, and it only costs twenty dollars or so.

In the meantime, do yourself a favor and open the window once in a while! In mild seasons, make sure your screens are securely in place and open a window on each end of the house on each floor and let that fresh air flow all the way through. Even in the winter, open one of the downstairs windows a crack—you may lose a little heat, but everyone will breathe better. If you're thinking of installing central air, you might consider an attic-mounted whole-house fan instead—it gives you whole-house ventilation as well as a cooling effect. Make sure your kitchen and bathroom fans work. And add some plants to your homescape. They add oxygen to the air and help remove harmful gases from it, and they aren't bad-looking either.

How can I get rid of that awful odor in my garbage disposal? #90

We misnamed these convenient kitchen helpers; we should have called them "garbage conditioners." They don't dispose of it; they grind and pulverize what you put in there so that the sewer system can dispose of it.

Odor in your disposal comes from clinging residue that hasn't moved through but is still in the disposal *rotting*. Once shredded, bits of food left lying in a disposal can very quickly grow a high bacteria count (especially meat scraps, etc.) How does this stuff get left in there? Some foods, like chicken bones, just don't grind up very well and shouldn't be put down a disposal. And the tough fibers in things like banana peels, corn husks, and celery wad up like nylon thread around the blades of a disposal and become a nesting ground for other food fragments. You can pour baking soda or vinegar and water solution in or grind some citrus peels or ice cubes through or even drop a disposal cleaning packet like Ajax Disposer Care in for temporary relief, but you need to treat the cause, not the symptom.

A disposal that does what it's designed to do shouldn't smell—here's how to make sure yours has a chance to do what it's supposed to. When you're running the disposal, always run oodles of water, like a whole sink full. Don't do like so many of us do, turn on the tap just before we turn on the disposal (and then shut the water off the second we switch off the disposal. When you run just this little bit of water in, it only sprays and wheezes and showers around in there. But when you run the disposal with a sink full of water it floods the chamber, forcing scraps and fragments against the walls and blades, really flushing the unit out. Once cleaned and flushed, it won't smell. If your disposal has been odoriferous for a while you might want to remove and disinfect the rubber drain baffle, then run some citrus peels through the unit to freshen it up. Then stick with your full flush campaign.

Sewer or drain systems, too, only function effectively in the presence of plenty of water flow. Too little water and those ground-up apple cores and onion skins won't be washed all the way to the main sewer—they'll settle down in your drainpipes to form a clog. Bacon fat and other greasy materials tossed down the drains can also give pipes hardening of the arteries. They close up and won't have the oomph to carry anything away. So don't dump the leftover gravy or the broiler pan drippings down the sink! And when you run anything through the disposal always follow it with one-minute flush of cold water, cold to keep any fat in what you're disposing of solid enough to be swept away.

How do I clean wicker, rattan, cane, or basketry ? #91

For much woven furniture that question will never need an answer because it will have broken down, frayed, and fallen apart by the time it gets dirty. To its discredit, we've brought the plant materials used to make wicker from the tropics, where they function very well, to parts of the world where they can't perform. The rattan stalk, for example, is a remarkably tough fiber, and it's been used for centuries in the tropical areas where it grows to make beautiful and extremely durable furniture. Left unfinished, it absorbs moisture from the air and maintains its strength and resilience forever. Imported to dryer climates, however, the fiber tends to dry out and shrink and become brittle, causing it to break and splinter. Raw rattan and cane can be wet down to restore the moisture, but water is often damaging to other components of woven furniture, and many pieces have paint or varnish finishes that make soaking impossible. All of this makes care of woven furniture a real problem in drier climates—it's difficult to clean, doesn't hold up well to use, and has innumerable nooks and crannies to harbor dust and cobwebs.

What we call wicker can be made from any of a variety of plant fibers, including rattan, cane, reed, willow, bamboo, and sea grass. Some wicker, such as "fiber rush," is even made of twisted paper. And some of the ingredients of wicker, such as rattan and reed, are the same plant called different things according to which part is used.

You can't treat all forms of wicker the same—how to clean it depends to some extent on what species of wicker it is and whether or not it's been varnished or painted, but the following general rules apply:

All forms of wicker should be vacuumed regularly to keep dust and cobwebs down. If the furnishing in question is unfinished wicker—that thin soft intricately woven stuff—or paper wicker—this is **all** that should be done by way of cleaning. Both paper and woven wicker are so hard to clean they should always be varnished or otherwise sealed to discourage dirt and stains.

When it gets visibly dirty, most other wicker can be damp wiped with a soft cloth dipped in a solution of mild cleaner and water. This means neutral cleaner, vegetable oil soap, or dish detergent, not harsh or strong chemicals or anything containing phosphates, which will only speed the disintegration of the sealer and of the fibers themselves. If the object is really grimy, you can use a soft brush with the mild soap solution to ream out all those little interstices.

All unfinished wicker (with the exception again of woven wicker and fiber rush) will benefit from an occasional mist or spray with water. This will restore some of the lost moisture and help keep it from getting brittle. Furniture polishes or oils, on the other hand, won't help moisturize but they will add an oily film that only attracts more dirt. You don't ever want to shower or soak finished wicker because the water will penetrate the tiny gaps in the finish and cause it to peel. Most baskets can be swished in hot dish detergent solution, then rinsed quickly in hot water and air dried. Don't let them soak—just a quick in and out, then tap them hard once or twice to knock off as much water as you can and set them out to air dry. If they warp, they can be dampened and re-formed, but must be held in place while drying to regain their shape.

Let all forms of wicker air dry well after cleaning before putting them back in service. Always try to position them, if at all possible, well away from heat sources and it wouldn't do them a bit of harm to keep company with a humidifier.

P.S. I knew a guy who was sure he'd found the ultimate solution to all stubborn cleaning problems—he bought a sandblaster! His very first target, of course, was the accumulated grime on his woven wicker love seat. Well, that stuff is so soft and brittle that before he could get the gun shut down all he had left was two hanging chains, eighty-four staples, four clamps, about eight hundred tiny nails, and nine pounds of sand and sawdust, in a pile on the porch—it was a clean pile.

How can I keep brass or copper from tarnishing  #92

Tarnishing is a process of "oxidation," which means the oxygen in the air actually joins with the surface molecules of the metal to form a dull coating of metal oxide on there. The presence of certain other compounds in the atmosphere, such as salt, sulfur, and good old H_2O, encourages the process. So the more you can limit or prevent the exposure of a metal surface to air and moisture and the elements, the less it will tarnish.

Most metal polishes leave a protective film of oil on the surface after they remove the layer of oxide that's accumulated, which helps discourage tarnishing. Coating freshly polished objects with auto wax, lemon oil, or a silicone protectant like Armor All or Beauty Seal will also retard tarnishing. If you want to use one of these, wash with warm detergent solution, rinse, and dry first to remove the oily coating left by the metal polish.

Many brass objects, such as lamps, hardware, and decorative grilles, are sprayed with clear lacquer right at the factory to keep air from reaching the metal and oxidizing it. The only trouble with this is that when the lacquer gets chipped or scratched, the exposed metal then tarnishes and leaves an ugly dark spot. The whole coat of lacquer then has to be stripped off and reapplied, which is a lot tougher than polishing uncoated metal.

But as long as lacquered brass or copper stays fully lacquered it will keep tarnish from forming. So don't leave lacquered things soaking in cleaning solutions, and you never want to use metal polish, abrasives, ammoniated cleaners, or even hot water on them. That coat of lacquer can be worn or peeled away more easily than you might imagine. Just dust and wipe with mild soap and water solution as needed.

For small objects like lamps, you can strip the lacquer yourself when necessary using lacquer thinner, acetone, or amyl acetate and super fine steel wool. Make sure you have good ventilation while you're doing it. Then you can use an aerosol can of clear lacquer to recoat the article. If it's a large or expensive or antique piece, though, better give the job to a pro.

Don't use any of these treatments for brass or copper used for food service.

The real question here is whether you want to waste a lot of time battling the nonstop and utterly inevitable process of oxidation. Does it really make sense to spend hours scrubbing something shiny, just to watch it redarken again? The way things naturally look is a lot easier standard to live with than "only bright is beautiful." Leave the polished brass to ships and hotels with twenty-four-hour polishing crews. One man's tarnish is another person's patina, after all.

Is there an easy way to wash a ceiling  #93

Not really easy, but there is a way! First—and it isn't just wishful thinking—they don't need to be washed much, except in a kitchen which collects airborne greases, and luckily most kitchens have a pretty small ceiling. Unlike a floor or wall, a ceiling doesn't get handprints, furniture marks, crayon scribbles, or animal abuse and it doesn't collect fuzzies or food spills. A bedroom or living room ceiling can go up to four years or more without being cleaned or painted . . . so relax! Occasional dusting with a long-handled lambswool duster or a vacuum brush attachment will help ceilings stretch out the span between cleanings. Lightly whisk away those grimy cobwebs as you go—don't crush or wipe them onto the ceiling.

Unless it's greasy or nicotine stained, a flat paint or acoustical-tile ceiling can be cleaned with a dry sponge. This is a piece of virgin rubber about five by seven inches and half an inch thick, very much like a giant eraser. It costs less than two dollars at a janitorial-supply store, and one sponge can often clean an entire ceiling in minutes. You just hold it folded in half in your hand and stroke it across the ceiling. Even if a ceiling needs to be washed, I often dry sponge it first, especially if it's heavily smoked or sooty, to remove all the loose surface dirt—this can triple the speed of ceiling washing afterward.

Some ceiling materials, such as sprayed-on acoustic ("cottage cheese") and heavy textures, are pretty much impossible to clean yourself. Professional ceiling cleaners can usually get acoustic materials surprisingly clean with their specialized oxidizing cleaners, or you can have the acoustic resprayed or painted.

Ceilings with gloss, semigloss, or satin enamel paint are washed with detergent and water as follows. Get yourself two buckets—one empty, the other with a solution of all-purpose cleaner. Dip an ordinary cellulose sponge only a quarter-inch into the solution in the bucket; then the solution won't run down your arm, down the crack of your back and into your shoes. It's also less likely to drip down the walls as you round those ceiling edges. Apply the solution to an area the size of your normal wing span and go over it twice, wringing the sponge into the empty bucket in between. Then polish the area you just cleaned with a dry towel. When you do it this way, all the dirt you take off goes into the "dirt" bucket, leaving the sponge and your cleaning solution fresh and clean to repeat the process.

Clean around the edges of the ceiling first, in as wide a swath as is comfortable. Then finish up the middle of the room. Overlap a couple of inches into the previously cleaned area when you polish the new area dry to feather out the edges and reduce the possibility of streaks.

For heavy accumulations of grease or nicotine use a heavy-duty cleaner or degreaser. And rinsing, which you do with a sponge dampened in clear water, may be necessary to avoid streaks.

Probably the single biggest help in washing ceilings is using a plank—yes, a wooden plank. Redwood is the best; it's light and strong. A two-foot-by-twelve-foot plank spanned between two ladders or a ladder and a sturdy plywood box (see illustration next page) gives you lots of room to move, and you can clean a quarter of a room or more without ever getting down. Always keep your cleaning tools and buckets on the

219

open end of the plank so you won't become so enthusiastic cleaning and looking up that you walk off the end of the plank.

Make yourself a sturdy box out of plywood for a safer and better way to reach high places. You can use it by itself or with a plank and sturdy step ladder to wash walls, paint ceilings, etc.

Don't forget to take the ceiling light fixture glass or diffuser down when you start and leave it soaking in dish detergent solution in the sink while you clean. When you finish the ceiling and while the plank is still up, you can just rinse the fixture off, wipe it dry, clamp it back up, and the whole job is done!

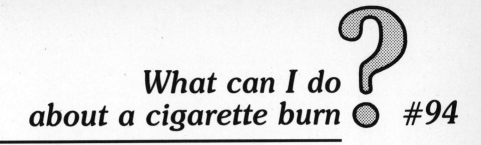

What can I do **?**
about a cigarette burn ● *#94*

Weep! Then contemplate your repair tactics, because cigarette burns are a *repair*, not a cleaning, problem. Burned floors, rugs, and countertops, alas, don't heal themselves like we humans do, so here's how to go about it:

Carpet. For surface damage, carefully trim off the burned tufts with a small, sharp pair of scissors. Rub the spot with fine, dry steel wool to remove as much of any remaining burned color as possible, then vacuum the area and spot-clean with detergent solution and rinse. Brush the pile as upright as you can when it dries. If this still leaves an unsightly hole, try snipping a few tufts from an inconspicuous place and glueing

221

them in with a little rubber cement or white glue. Put a tiny puddle of the glue in the bottom of the hole and let it get slightly tacky before you artfully place the tuft tidbits on top. Make sure the glue is good and dry before putting any furniture back or opening the area up to traffic.

If the burn is beyond this treatment, have a professional carpet repairman cut a plug from your saved remnants or the closet floor and patch it in.

Upholstery. Lightly rub with dry steel wool, then spot-clean with detergent solution and rinse. If a hole remains, darn with matching thread and then iron the spot, using a damp press cloth. For a high-napped fabric like synthetic plush, you might try sticking a bit of backing material in through the hole and sewing it in place around the hole, then glueing a little plush patch in on top of it. You can probably swipe some patch material from the underside or the back. Or if the hole is in the right place and you don't socialize much with mathematicians you can simply have the furniture people add another of those lovely little buttons.

Wood Furniture and Floors. If the burn is confined to the finish, rub the burned varnish away with a cotton swab moistened with nonoily fingernail polish remover. Don't get the remover outside the area of the burn. Then apply clear nail polish—test first—or polyurethane varnish over it.

If the wood itself is affected, gently scrape, then sand your way down to bare wood—then restain and re-finish with whatever clear finish was on there originally. A couple of extra coats of the varnish or finish applied to the area of the injury alone can help disguise a small dip or depression.

If the hole is really deep, look for a colored wood filler or wax furniture repair stick that comes as close as possible to the surface color, then apply according to the manufacturer's instructions and revarnish. You'll probably want to put the repair of deep damage on fine or expensive furniture in the hands of a pro.

Counters

Formica—Scrub the burned area only with powdered cleanser, then polish the spot with appliance wax to restore the luster.

Cultured marble or Corian—lightly sand out the burn with 200–300 grit sandpaper, then use progressively finer grades of sandpaper to smooth out the scratches, finishing with 600 or 800 grit. Then polish with auto rubbing compound and wax with car wax.

Vinyl Flooring. Scrub the burned area only with fine wet steel wool and powdered cleanser, then rinse the spot well, dry, and apply a coat of floor wax or finish.

P.S. At least there's something positive to think about while you're doing all this—how lucky you are that the whole place didn't go up in smoke.

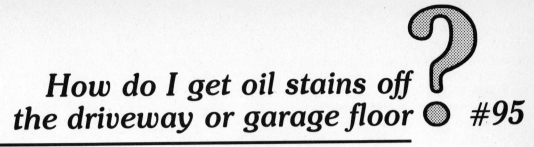

How do I get oil stains off the driveway or garage floor ? ● #95

There isn't anything uglier or more obvious than a black oil stain on a light-colored garage floor or driveway. Stains are a pain because they not only look bad, but things like oil dripping from a car can be tracked throughout the house or yard in minutes.

There are special concrete cleaners available from janitorial-supply stores for removing oil, rust, and other stains from concrete. If you have a seriously stained floor, you may want to consider using one of these. For most of us, the simple strategies that follow will do fine.

If it's a fresh oil spot, throw on a handful of kitty litter, which is actually what mechanics use to soak up oil, only they have other names for it like Floor Dry, and grind it in with your foot. Let it sit there a few hours to absorb the oil, then sweep it up.

For old, hard spots, scrape what you can off the surface first with a putty knife. Any petroleum solvent such as paint thinner will then break down and dissolve the stain, and you can use a paper towel or disposable cloth to remove most of it. If you want to go further than that, place a poultice made of crushed kitty litter or sawdust mixed with paint thinner or mineral spirits on it. Put a damp cloth over it to keep the solvent from evaporating too fast. The "sponge" effect of the poultice will draw the oil out. After a few hours, remove the poultice and let the area dry—only a slight stain will remain. Much of even this can be removed by scrubbing the spot with a solution of powdered laundry detergent (Tide) and hot water.

Once the spots are removed, I'd scrub the whole floor with a strong Tide solution, rinse well and dry, and put on a couple coats of acrylic concrete seal. If concrete is left raw it not only stains, but the surface constantly wears away and produces dust and grit every time you sweep it. We professionals learned quick, where any amount of concrete is involved, to seal it. That is, apply several protective coats of shiny sealer that acts as a shield for the concrete so that stains, dirt, and moisture can't penetrate it. The seal also presents a smooth, slick surface that can be swept or dust mopped in minutes. Sealer can even make floors on which stains still remain look better. To ensure a good bond between the sealer and the surface, etch the floor with an acid floor etching agent before you apply the sealer. Once it's sealed, removal of spots and spills is no sweat. And it'll be so pretty, you'll have goose bumps!

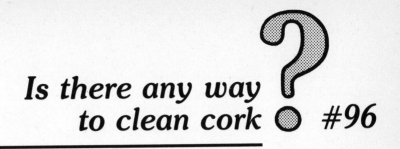

Is there any way to clean cork **?** ○ #96

Cork is by very nature soft, crumbly, porous, and absorbent, so if it gets all stained and gross don't expect a miracle. Cork has some marvelous qualities, but it's not a particularly good material for maintenance-free living.

For cork wall tiles, bulletin boards, wall coverings, etc.

• Run the upholstery head of your vacuum over it first to pick up all the dust and sloughed off cork bits.

• Then dry sponge it. The chemically treated rubber dry sponge,

225

available at janitorial-supply stores, will pull off any surface soil or smudges.

For impregnated soil

• Don't spray cleaning solution directly onto cork, or the liquid will be absorbed into the cork and only drive the soil deeper.

• Instead wipe the surface carefully with a sponge or cloth dampened with all-purpose cleaner. Then squeeze your sponge or cloth as dry as you can and go back over the surface to remove the solution.

Never lean a ladder or other cleaning tools against cork, or you'll leave a lasting first impression!

For cork floors

The same cautions apply to cork as to wood floors:

• Go easy on water—unsealed cork floors are easily damaged by flooding. Cool water can be used sparingly on sealed cork, if the water is picked up quickly and the floor dried promptly. Spirit waxes or solvent paste waxes are better for the floor than water emulsion finishes.

• If you don't want your cork tiles to loosen, crack, warp, whiten, stain, or turn grainy or brittle, don't use harsh alkaline cleaners, ammonia, abrasives, oil sweeping compounds, or strong solvents such as paint thinner or lacquer thinner on them.

• Keep grit swept or dust mopped up so it can't abrade the finish, and pick up spills promptly with a lightly dampened mop.

• Use coasters under furniture legs to help avoid indentations.

If the floor is finished with paste wax—clean and polish with fresh paste wax, using a steel wool pad on a floor polisher.

If the floor is finished with urethane—lightly sand any worn areas and recoat with urethane.

Cork floors can be sanded down and refinished like any wood floor, but go easy—this particular "wood" is so soft it can be oversanded very easily.

Is there any fast way to dust bookcases and bookshelves ? #97

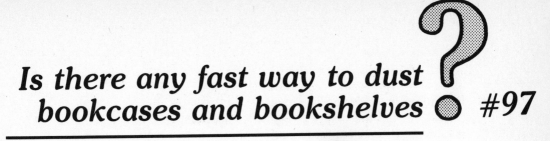

I don't know about fast, but there is a **better** way. "Dusty" seems to be the natural condition of bookcases, but dust doesn't do them any good—it only speeds the deterioration of books and bindings. So no matter how long we can manage to ignore it, there comes a time when we want to remove it. Here you can't use the slightly damp cloth that can be used to such advantage elsewhere, because it could stain or permanent wave the covers, jackets, or edges of the books. A vacuum is the best tool for the purpose—the dusting brush or crevice tool of a canister vacuum or a handheld vac. Anything else—especially a feather duster—just redistributes the dust rather than disposing of it. Lacking a vacuum, the next best thing is a cloth like the New Pig (see p. 56), which catches and holds the dust by electrostatic attraction, not oily, and potentially staining, dust treatments.

For a once-over-lightly regular dusting, just stick the vacuum attachment in and vacuum across the tops of the books. If you put your books on the shelf the way the professionals, librarians and booksellers, do—all spines aligned right up with the edge of the shelf—there won't be any exposed ledge to worry about. And those mildew-prone books will have better air circulation behind them, too. Twice a year or so, after you've done the tops, grab three or four of the books at a time, tip them backward, and dust the shelf underneath with your other hand. If you want to pull an individual book out to dust it, don't just grab the top edge with your finger and tip it out. The book's backbone, or binding, which can be quite brittle on older books especially, will last a lot longer if you put your hand behind and slide the whole book out.

If you're feeling downright saintly or moving or redecorating, so you have no choice, you can tackle the whole shelf and treat each book to a really thorough dusting. Just be forewarned that your little library will seem to have swelled to at least twice its size the minute you pull those innocent-looking volumes off the shelves. After you get them all out, pick them up one by one, firmly, to keep the pages tightly closed, and vacuum all sides. When you do the top and bottom always dust outward from the spine, to avoid shoving dust down into the binding. Then vacuum the whole case vigorously while you have the chance and whisk away any mouse droppings, mash notes, old newspaper clippings, lost cassette tapes, aged *Playboys*, or pint bottles that were hidden back behind there. Don't forget the top and sides and incredibly dusty back of the bookcase while you're at it. You can wipe the case down with a damp cloth, too, if it's painted metal or well sealed or imitation wood. Just make sure those shelves are good and dry before you start stacking your valuable volumes back onto them. If you want to put furniture polish on your wooden bookcase, a wax type is much safer for the books than an oil type.

When you put all the books back in, try not to cram them together so tightly this time—the strongarm act of getting them in and out under such circumstances is pretty brutalizing to jackets, covers, and bindings.

Enclosed bookshelves, of course, are the ultimate answer to this time-consuming chore. And even if you can't afford that, every several years or so you can take a good hard look over those shelves and consider eliminating the books you don't want or need. The only action many books see, all those volumes we keep for "show" or vanity, is when they're dusted. If you never crack it—you don't like it; you're not interested in it; it's hopelessly out of date—get rid of it. There are less dust-catching ways to impress people.

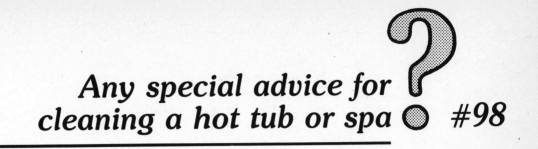

Any special advice for cleaning a hot tub or spa ⬤ *#98*

Having a hot tub or spa is kind of like fulfilling our lifetime dream of owning our own little pond or creek. There's one big difference, however—nature controls and cleans up the creek, but that fiberglass and plastic relaxin' hole at home is all ours, even if we never get time to use it.

The water in it, too, isn't like nature's water, which is constantly aerated, filtered, and cleansed as it burbles over the rocks and gravel of the stream. Even good water does bad things when it's contaminated, as spa water is constantly, with body oils, perspiration, suntan lotion, cosmetics, and excess minerals. And then kept steadily at a temperature almost ideal for bacteria breeding. So to prevent cleaning problems you have to become a bit of a water chemist. You can get a water testing kit at your spa dealers and the chemicals you need to keep water conditions copacetic. The dealer can also advise you as to the concentrations of various things you want in your particular spa's water.

Then you can check pH, mineral, and sanitizer (chlorine) levels several times a week and adjust as necessary. If you faithfully maintain these key measurements at the recommended levels, you can avoid or minimize such problems as scale buildup, bacteria and algae growth, clogged pipes and filters, and corroded spa components.

To keep water clean and clear, you'll also want to run the pump two hours a day, whether you use the spa or not. And check and clean out the skimmer basket and pump strainer at least once a week. Super chlorinate the water once a week, too, to kill any lingering algae or bacteria and destroy any organic wastes that haven't been filtered out. Clean filters as needed and add defoamer, water clarifier, or other specialty chemicals as necessary—your owner's manual will tell you what and when—to keep the water clean and inviting. If a "bathtub ring" forms at the water line—it shouldn't if you're keeping careful track of those water conditions—wipe it away with Spa Gloss or a similar cleaner that will dissolve the scum without interfering with the action of the water treatment chemicals.

Every month or so, drain the spa and clean with a scrubbing sponge and mild detergent, or your favorite **nonabrasive** cleaner. A 3M #63 white-backed scrubbing sponge will never hurt the surface as long as you keep it wet. Use no powdered cleansers, steel wool, or colored nylon scrub pads, which can scratch and dull the finish. If there is a bit of hard-water buildup on there, a good phosphoric acid cleaner (see p. 80) should get rid of it. But if you're keeping the water properly treated, none of these more drastic measures should be needed. Rinse off all soap and detergent when you're through and use Spa Fast Gloss or a similar silicone sealer and polish to restore the luster and add a layer of protective finish. If all this sounds like a lot of work, at least we can head for the hot tub when it's over.

P.S. If you keep your tub testing and cleaning tools in a kit or basket right on site, it'll encourage you to do the job right and timely.

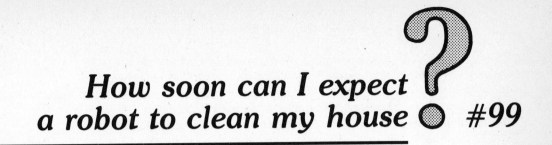

How soon can I expect a robot to clean my house ? ● #99

I have a dream—just like you—that someday we'll have self-cleaning toilets and a vacuum that automatically zooms through the house once I've left for work in the morning. I have a dream of a self-changing diaper, too—o.k., so maybe that one's a nightmare—but it's a fact that for sale right now at your local hardware store is a light that turns itself off when you leave the room—controls to turn down the heat after you go to bed, warm the house and start the oatmeal before you get up, answer the phone, and monitor security while you're away, even detect and report fires and emergencies! We're already seeing homes with central systems management computers installed that regulate the functioning of everything in the house from heating and cooling to entertainment systems. These built-in brains can be programmed and instructed by keypad, by voice command, or by telephone from another location. The obvious next step is appliances controlled by voice alone, which will even be able to answer you and ask questions if they need to. Washing machines, dishwashers, and cooking and food processing appliances able to make routine operating decisions on their own should be common by the mid-1990s. And there's 1001 other computerized household items being researched and developed right now. So what's so farfetched about robot to do the things we hate?

Just fifteen years ago, a "personal computer" would have taken up an entire room of the house—today it's a typewriter-size machine in the corner that many of us think of as our right arm. We've already got robots that can clean swimming pools, shear sheep, fight fires, deliver mail, dive in deep water, and handle toxic wastes—surely they can make one to tackle the green hairies in the refrigerator. Hang in there another fifteen years and we may see a robot capable of taking out the trash, washing the mini blinds, organizing the closet, and—yes—matching the socks!

Interestingly enough, some of the most mundane chores require the most sophisticated robotics. You and I have always known the finesse it takes to get in, under, and around with a twenty-four-pound roaring vacuum without clipping, bumping, or smashing into things or slurping up anything you didn't intend to. We've already got robotic floor scrubbers and vacuum cleaners to do large unobstructed areas like supermarket aisles and corridors, but they're like a bull in a china shop for a crowded room. Major strides will have to be made in the intelligence, "eyesight," and manual dexterity of existing machines before they can do a lot of the stuff you and I can do while daydreaming!

Keep dreaming of a robot to do all the laundry, cooking, and cleaning, as well as baby-sit, balance the checkbook, write our thank-you notes, water the lawn, watch the house, and feed the parakeet—a governess, butler, and maid all wrapped up in one. We'll probably see it by the year 2000. For today's harried homemakers it sounds almost too good to be true. In reality, it'll probably be like everything else—getting the model with all the options you want will put you 200 percent over budget!

How do I clean the moosehead ? ● #100

Wondered if I'd ever get around to it, didn't you . . .

"But I'll **never** own a moosehead or anything similar." So thought I and millions of others who now have a mounted rack, head, or hide hung on a wall or tucked away in a back room, attic, or basement somewhere. How many hunters do you know? They'll all average at least one preserved piece in their lifetime and will probably will it to you. I don't even hunt anymore, and I have two, an antelope head from Dad and a wood duck my wife surprised me with one Christmas. Cleaning these once in a lifetime works of art starts with where you put them.

You won't often have to clean the cougar if you pick the right place for him in the house. All the cleaning skills in the world will never restore damage or abuse. So forget about any spot near a fireplace or wood-burning stove or any source of heat or soot or where cigarette smoke collects or grease from the kitchen can easily drift. Stay way from direct sunlight, too, or your black bear or hartebeest will soon be sun bleached.

Anywhere kids and company can reach and touch is a poor choice, too. Cats and dogs, too—cats especially—can attack and shred a specimen faster than sulfuric acid in your cleaning solution.

Many taxidermists are only too happy to come to your home and do the initial placing of the piece for you—after all, keeping their work winsome is in their interest, too.

The ideal location, according to award-winning taxidermy artist Richard Jeppsen, is a glass case. "For birds and white animals it's nothing less than essential. A glass case at least triples the life of a mount. It saves cleaning time and you can relax when visitors come. You can also use the glass case as a diorama to depict the animal in a real-life setting." The cost of a case is usually incidental compared to the price of what you're protecting. A case will keep out preserved creatures' two worst predators: kids and pets. After all, your own brood might be trained to "hands off," but what about their friends and visitors? Kids with bows and arrows and BB guns will even shoot a specimen—it happens a lot! And the only cleaning an enclosed animal needs is a spritz of window cleaner and a wipe with a soft cloth!

If your trophy isn't under glass, though, the next thing you need to do is dust. There's more dust in the house where they are now than in the jungle or forest where they once roamed. For this you can take a feather duster to them about once a week, carefully flicking with the flow of hair or feathers—never against! Hair is hollow like straw and gets brittle, and if you bend it a few times it'll break. You can use your vacuum, too, but only on a lower blower setting—never suction. You could also use a blow dryer on cool—never hot! A large game animal can also be wiped gently in the direction of the hair with a soft cloth. Don't handle the hair at all, even with clean hands; when you're moving the animal, pick it up by the horns or base. A fingerprint on any mount may not be apparent immediately, but as soon as the dust settles in it'll show. You can carefully realign the hair when necessary with a soft brush or a fine wire dog grooming brush, working again, in the direction of the fur. You can hit the horns, nose, and teeth with a slightly dampened cloth, but any water whatsoever on the fur or skin can stretch it out of shape. Glass eyes can be cleaned with glass cleaner.

Birds can't be brushed or wiped—those exquisitely arranged and overlapped little feather patterns are unlikely to emerge intact.

"Shiny" horns are out of style right now, but if you have that sort of mount a tiny bit of baby oil applied with a small soft cloth will brighten them back up. Don't ever use any solvent around mounted animals, especially fish, which are usually painted with lacquer. Most lacquered lunkers can tolerate a window cleaning solution or alcohol wipe or, if in doubt, at least a gentle onceover with a damp cloth and a couple of cotton swabs.

Every ten or fifteen years or so, when it comes time for deep cleaning, a thorough, safe job of it can only be done by the taxidermist who originally created the trophy. They usually put their name and address right on the critter somewhere. If this is impossible, you can take it to another taxidermist, but he or she will probably make you sign a waiver releasing them if any damage is done. Since they have no way of knowing what tanning process or treatments were used in the initial mounting, it's hard for them to match the cleaning accordingly.

What about the water buffalo hide? If you have or inherit a fur rug or skin try to keep it on the wall—walking or rolling on a bearskin or zebra hide will not only soil it beyond cleaning, but damage or deteriorate the hair. Hanging rugs should be taken down once a year and dusted in the direction of the fur, again, blowing with cool air from a vacuum set on blower or a hair dryer. **Never** put a rug like this in the washer. They can be dry cleaned, but the backing has to be removed first, and this is often more bother and expense than it's worth.

My Favorite Cleaning Tools

Here's a chart illustrating some of the basic professional tools, equipment and supplies that make housekeeping faster and easier. Most of these can be found at a janitorial-supply store.

Item	Description	Source/Type	
neutral cleaner	A cleaner gentle enough to be safe for almost any surface because it's pH neutral—neither acid nor alkaline.	Available in concentrated form at janitorial-supply stores—or you can simply use hand dishwashing detergent.	
alcohol-based window cleaner	A fast-drying, streak-free cleaner for glass, chrome, and other small areas and hard surfaces	Available in concentrated form at janitorial-supply stores or in supermarkets as Windex, etc.	
degreaser	An aggressively alkaline cleaner that cuts quickly through oily soils and grease deposits.	Janitorial-supply stores (butyl cleaner or a product called Soilmaster).	
spray bottle	Professional-quality trigger sprayer bottle such as Continental brand, in quart or 22-oz. size. Fill with cleaning solutions you mix up yourself from concentrate.	Janitorial-supply store.	

Item	Description	Source/Type	
sponge	The best sponge for most general cleaning purposes is a cellulose sponge in a size that fits your hand comfortably.	Widely available.	
scrub sponge	White nylon-backed cellulose sponge is a safe scrubber for almost any surface. Green and all other colors of nylon scrubber should only be used on nondamageable surfaces and with great care.	Supermarkets, discount stores, and janitorial-supply stores.	
cleaning cloth	Thick absorbent terry cloth sewn into a sturdy tube shape that gives you sixteen fresh surfaces to clean, dry, and polish with.	Make your own (see p. 175); also available by mail from the Cleaning Center.	
utility brush	The handle on this brush keeps your knuckles out of the nasties and the nylon bristles and bristle bed won't crack, rot, mildew, or go mushy.	Janitorial-supply store.	
disinfectant cleaner	Quaternary disinfectant, one of the safer germ killers for home use, with detergent built right in so it cleans and sanitizes at the same time.	Available at janitorial-supply stores in concentrated form and in supermarkets (products with ammonium chloride listed among the label ingredients).	
disposable dust cloth	Built-in dust treatment or electrostatic action attracts and holds the dust.	Electrostatic and treated cloths (such as Masslinn) available at janitorial-supply stores.	

Item	Description	Source/Type
lambswool duster	The lambswool head grips dust by static attraction; the long handle lets you do even high and low dusting with ease. Extension handles also available.	Janitorial supply or discount store.
dry sponge	Chemically treated 5″ × 7″ rubber pad that removes dirt film, smoke, and nongreasy soils from acoustic ceilings, flat painted walls, lampshades, etc.	Janitorial-supply store.
vegetable oil soap	A mild vegetable oil-based soap for cleaning wood surfaces safely.	Supermarket or janitorial-supply store (Murphy's Oil Soap or Lin-Sol).
angle broom	Professional-quality angle broom with exploded tip nylon bristles.	Janitorial-supply store.
push broom	24″ head with handle brace and nylon bristles: a ring of coarse bristles around the outside and finer bristles inside.	Janitorial-supply store.
mats	Professional-quality "walkoff" mats for every entranceway: synthetic turf outside the door, rubber backed nylon or olefin inside the door.	Janitorial-supply store.

Item	Description	Source/Type
dustmop	Professional-quality cotton dust mop with 18-inch head and swivel handle.	Janitorial-supply store.
dustmop treatment	A special oil you apply to a dust mop head to increase its pickup power.	Janitorial-supply store.
hand floor scrubber	Long-handled tool for fast easy scrubbing of floors, baseboards, any large surfaces. Interchangeable wax applicator and dust mop heads available.	Department store, janitorial-supply store, and Cleaning Center
floor finish ("wax")	Professional-quality, non-yellowing, self-polishing floor finish such as Johnson's Complete or Top Gloss.	Janitorial-supply store.
wax stripper	Professional-quality rinseless wax stripper for quick removal of stubborn buildups.	Janitorial-supply store.
phosphoric acid cleaner	Professional-strength phosphoric acid cleaner for speedy removal of hard water scale.	Janitorial-supply store.
bowl cleaner, swab and caddy	Extra-strength phosphoric acid formula for hard water deposits in toilets; cotton or synthetic swab head is better than a brush for cleaning the bowl and applying bowl cleaners; caddy stores it all neatly together.	Janitorial-supply store.

Item	Description	Source/Type
pumice bar	Block of pumice stone for removal of toilet bowl ring (always wet before using!).	Janitorial-supply store.
upright vacuum	Professional-quality 6-amp model with 12″ head, beater bar and a long cord.	Janitorial-supply store.
squeegee	Professional-quality brass squeegee with 10″, 12″, or 14″ blade. The fastest and best way to do windows.	Janitorial-supply store (Ettore Steccone is a good brand).
extension pole	Lightweight aluminum pole that extends from four to eight feet to enable you to reach high windows easily.	Janitorial-supply store

Index

Scrub brushes, 15–16, 42, 145; right way to use, 16, 42
Scrub sponge or scrub pad, nylon, 15–16, 21, 26, 27, 50, 70, 73, 78, 80, 91, 104, 132, 164, 173, 199, 230, 237
Sea grass, cleaning, 214
Sealing to prevent stains and ease cleaning, 22, 23, 24, 42, 55, 107, 155, 203, 214, 224
Silk flowers and plants, how to clean, 157–59
"Skip" cleaning, 109
Smoke odor and stain removing, 106–107, 169–71, 143
Soap scum
  prevention, 72–73
  removal, 68, 73, 79–80, 230
Soft water, advantages for cleaning, 58–59
Soil retardants, 162
Soot
  prevention, 55–56
  removal from rooms and furnishings, 169–71, 202–203, 219; from stone or masonry, 106–107
Spas, cleaning, 229–30
Sponge
  best type of cleaning, 40, 237
  how to clean, 145
  versus cloth for cleaning, 39–40, 119
Spot cleaning, 35, 40, 76, 161, 162
Spray bottles for cleaning, pro pointers for using, 87–89, 94; best kind to get, 88, 236
Squeegee, 12, 18, 71, 73, 104, 128, 153, 198, 199, 240
Started cleaning, how to get, 1–3
Stickers, removing, 90–92
Storage of cleaning supplies and equipment, 69–71
Stripper, wax, 10, 96, 239
Stripping wax or floor finish, 7–8, 37–38, 75, 156
Stuffed animals; how to clean, 135–36
Suede cleaning, 186

T

Tar removal, 178
Textured ceilings and walls, cleaning, 118–119
Time fragments, fitting cleaning into, 4–6
Toilet bowl ring, removing, 80
toothbrush, old, as scrub brush, 16, 111, 187
Toys, soft; how to clean, 135–36
Traffic patterns, in a home; how they affect cleaning, 14, 74
Trophies, hunting; how to clean, 233–35
TSP, 35, 164

Tub and tile cleaner. *See* Acid cleaners
Two-bucket system of cleaning, 21–22, 28, 119, 219

U

Unnecessary cleaning, 18, 45, 74–76
Urine stains and odor, how to remove, 67–68
Utility brush, 16, 178, 237

V

Varsity Contractors, 247
Vegetable oil soap, 21–22, 42, 214, 238
Vinegar as a cleaner, 104, 137–38, 185, 212
  as a deodorizer, 138
  as a rinsing agent, 96, 138, 159, 165
Vacuum
  bag, when to change, 101–102; cleaning or replacing, 32, 56, 102
  beater bar, 33, 64, 84, 146, 161
  cordless or handheld, 83–84, 136, 161, 203, 227
  least dust-producing type, 56
  suction, reasons for reduced, 32–33
  wet/dry, 82, 136, 162
Vomit stains and odor, removing, 67–68

W

Wallpaper and wall covering
  cleaning, 204–205
  grease stains on, 205
Walls, textured, cleaning, 118–119
Washwater, when to change, 28–29
Waterless cleaners, 179
Water stains on ceilings, removing, 206–207
Water temperature and cleaning, 133–34
Wax or floor finish, 35
  applying, 8, 38, 95–96
  best type to use, 51–53, 75, 239
  paste type, 51, 52, 154–56, 226, 227
  reasons for using, 52
Wicker, how to clean and preserve, 213–15
Willow, cleaning, 214
windows, 75
  cleaning frame and sill and tracks, 198–99
  cleaning at night, 62
  cleaning outside of, 152–53
Wood floors, how to clean and shine, 154–56
Woodstove mess prevention, 202–203
Wood, using water on, 21, 22, 41–42, 134, 145, 155
Woodwork, cleaning, 41–42
Woolite, 81, 136, 158

244

About the Author

"Aw, come on, you don't really clean anymore," is the most common response author Don Aslett gets when he introduces himself. Those who know his nine highly successful books, his nationally acclaimed cleaning company, Varsity Contractors, Inc., and his TV and radio reputation know that his media title of "America's No. 1 Cleaning Expert" is no exaggeration—nor is it a matter of mere theory. His authority to speak out boldly about cleaning comes from thirty-two years on the job cleaning and operating a professional cleaning business beginning as a college freshman in 1957 at Idaho State University. For more than a decade now his overwhelming objective has been to raise the image and awareness of cleaning in this country and to help the homemaker, male or female, be a happier and more efficient cleaner. His humorous, highly visual, and motivational approach to even the most mundane topics has enabled him to enrich millions of lives throughout the U.S. and Canada and abroad. Nothing is ever past tense about a Don Aslett production—**he is doing** what he writes and talks about. He still owns and manages several businesses related to home and commercial cleaning and proudly claims possession of the best and fastest-growing cleaning museum and cleaning library in the world. He's also a consultant to the business community on cleaning and maintenance-free design and a highly sought after speaker and seminar leader, having delivered over three thousand public presentations in the last thirty years. His million-plus copies sold of cleaning books begins with *Is There Life After Housework?* in 1981, and also includes *Do I Dust or Vacuum First?, Clutter's Last Stand, Who Says it's a Woman's Job to Clean?, Make Your House Do the Housework, Pet Clean-Up Made Easy,* and *Cleaning Up for a Living.* His books have been selections of major book clubs and translated into French, German, Danish, and Dutch as well as being perennial paperback bestsellers in the U.S., Canada, England, and Australia. And his answer to, "Do you still clean anymore?" is "Yes, every day, every chance I get—nothing restores order and dignity to human life like the act of caring for what we use."

Don and his wife Barbara live on a sixty-acre ranch outside Pocatello, Idaho, and spend part of the year in Kauai, Hawaii.

Where to Write For   All of the professional cleaning products and tools mentioned in this book can be found at janitorial-supply stores. Look in the *Yellow Pages* under "Janitorial Supplies." But if the nearest store is halfway across the state, you can get supplies by mail-order by writing to Don Aslett's Cleaning Center, PO Box 39-M, Pocatello, ID 83204 (phone: 208-232-6212). All of Don's earlier books plus a fast-paced, ninety-minute videotape are available here, too. Call or write for a catalog.